"This is a powerful book full of e
scriptures and exceptional encouragement for the soul. It is a
humble, heartfelt offering of hope from true spiritual friends.
Can Jesus Get A Witness? is sure to serve as a source of strength, support, and solace for many. I highly recommend it."

Earl Grant Jr., Ph.D.
Senior Pastor-Teacher, Covenant Community Church
San Antonio, TX

"Using poetic, powerful, and persuasive prose, Fredricc and Kan'Dace Brock remind and exhort all Christians to recognize the victorious redemption of Jesus at work in our lives and to respond to Jesus' call to serve as His witnesses in a hurting world. These biblically sound, strikingly relevant, and deeply inspiring sermons will bless all who read them."

Andrew Arterbury, Ph.D.
Associate Professor of Christian Scriptures
George W. Truett Theological Seminary
Baylor University

"We are living in an age of apostasy when preaching about Christ. Cross, Calvary, and Conversion is seemingly unpopular and out of season. Reverends Fredricc and Kan'Dace Brock have given us an anointed compilation of twenty powerful, prolific, and practical messages that are sure to inspire and empower Christians everywhere to stand up and be a witness for the Lord! OMG, what a great resource tool for the advancement of God's Kingdom!"

Drs. Michael and Tamara Scott
MTS Ministries, Inc.

"This rich and transformative volume of sermons by preachers Fredricc and Kan'Dace Brock are grounded in the Bible, embody sound theology, and lend themselves to practical application. These creative voices of the 21st century know what it means to be a witness for Jesus and boldly show others the way. I highly recommend this work to all who need a word from the Lord."

Rev. Richelle B. White, Ph.D.
Professor of Youth Ministry
Kuyper College

"I am thrilled to encourage you to read this incredible book that will change your life! Kan'Dace & Fredricc Brock are two very accomplished individuals and I am grateful to have had them minister with our global ministry at athletic events. Their passion to see lives changed is evident and as powerful as their testimony."

Dr. Sam Mings
President & Founder, Lay Witnesses for Christ International

"Fredricc and Kan'Dace Brock's *Can Jesus Get a Witness?* is an inspiring and insightful expression of the soulful style of preaching, which has been the hallmark of the historical African-American Church for centuries. You will hear the preacher's cadence, his voice rising and falling, taking you back to the traditional 'celebration' time of preaching on every page. These two visionaries and emerging exegetical giants will compel thinkers to think more deeply, and preachers to preach with a renewed level of passion, grace, and Spirit-filled excellence. I am grateful to be in covenant friendship with them both and couldn't be more excited to offer my support and endorsement than I am now!"

John Moreland, M.Div.
Senior Servant, Denver Christian Bible Church
Affiliate Faculty, Colorado Christian University

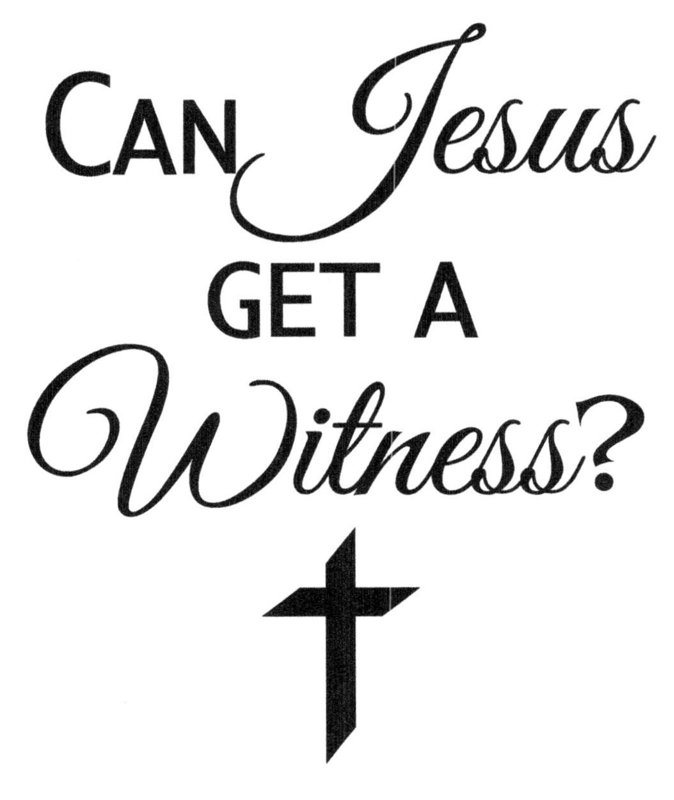

Sermons to Move You to Action

FREDRICC & KAN 'DACE BROCK

TOUCH PUBLISHING

ISBN: 978-1-942508-07-6

Scripture quoted taken from the King James Version.

Published by Touch Publishing
P.O. Box 180303
Arlington, TX 76096
www.TouchPublishingServices.com

Cover design by Touch Publishing

Fredricc Gerard Brock Ministries
To connect with Pastor Fredricc or Lady Kan'Dace Brock visit
www.fgbministries.com

Library of Congress Control Number: 2015941502

Printed in the United States of America on acid-free paper

1 Thomas G. Long, *The Witness of Preaching, 2nd ed.* (Louisville: Westminster/John Knox Press, 2005), 52.

2 Haddon W. Robinson, *Biblical Preaching: The Development and Delivery of Expository Messages, 2nd ed.* (Grand Rapids: Baker Academic, 2008), 27.

3 Ralph D. West, "Weaving the Textual Web". In Cleophus J. LaRue, editor, *Power in the Pulpit: How America's Most Effective Black Preachers Prepare Their Sermons* (Westminster/John Knox Press, 2002), 176.

4 Robert Smith Jr., *Doctrine That Dances: Bringing Doctrinal Preaching and Teaching to Life* (Nashville: B&H Academic, 2008), 4.

Messages

1- Can Jesus Get a Witness? by Fredricc Brock	1
2- A Formula for Victory by Fredricc Brock	11
3- Don't Be Bitter, Be Better by Fredricc Brock	17
4- God's Presence Makes the Difference by Fredricc Brock	25
5- Praise in the Middle of a Blackout by Kan'Dace Brock	33
6- God Will Work it Out by Fredricc Brock	41
7- He'll Bring You Out of Lodebar by Fredricc Brock	49
8- God Don't Need No Matches by Fredricc Brock	57
9- Forgiveness at the Cross by Fredricc Brock	65
10- Giving God Your Best by Kan'Dace Brock	73
11- Dealing with Divine Delays by Fredricc Brock	79
12- A Theology of Suffering by Fredricc Brock	87
13- I Still Trust Him by Fredricc Brock	97
14- Anguish at the Cross by Fredricc Brock	103
15- Marred in His Hands by Fredricc Brock	111
16- Directions in the Middle of a Mess-Up by Fredricc Brock	117
17- What to Expect When You're Expecting by Fredricc Brock	123
18- I'm Moving Forward by Fredricc Brock	131
19- Weep No More by Fredricc Brock	137
20- Making a Choice to Live Chosen by Fredricc Brock	141

1 - Can Jesus Get A Witness?

"And Jesus came and spake unto them, saying, All power is given unto me in heaven and in earth. Go ye therefore, and teach all nations, baptizing them in the name of the Father, and of the Son, and of the Holy Ghost: Teaching them to observe all things whatsoever I have commanded you: and, lo, I am with you always, even unto the end of the world. Amen."

Matthew 28:18-20

I LOVE THE old-school television courtroom who-done-its. I grew up watching Perry Mason and Matlock. And, y'all, in every courtroom drama show I watched, they would undoubtedly at some point present someone who is called a "witness." In the court of law, a witness is somebody who has direct knowledge of an important event. You may or may not realize this, but in court, a witness takes an oath before speaking and is expected to tell "the truth, the whole truth, and nothing but the truth"—even when it seems like folks can't handle the truth. If you know anything about a good courtroom show, you'll know that there are three main types of witnesses.

First of all, there is the 'eyewitness.' Eyewitnesses are good to have because they're not depending on what "that guy over there" said happened—they saw it with their own eyes and they're willing to tell what they saw.

Secondly, you have the 'expert witness.' Now, an expert witness may not have seen what happened like the eyewitness did, but an expert witness has a lot of knowledge on the topic in question.

Then lastly, there is the 'character witness.' A character witness may not have seen what happened like the eyewitness, and may not know all about the topic in question like the expert witness, but a character witness can vouch for the reputation of a person involved in the case.

As I look across the landscape of this postmodern society I see a world where everything seems to be brought into question. We live in a world where some folks doubt if God is real, and the folks who know God is real sometimes doubt if His power is real. In this context, as we consider keeping God's vision in perspective, I want to ask the question: **Can Jesus get a witness?**

In a world where:

- 50% of marriages end in divorce,
- people are concerned about the outcome and discouraged by their income,
- recession has taken over our homes,
- depression has taken over our minds,
- and obsession has taken over our bodies,

Can Jesus get a witness to tell somebody that the cross is still vacant, the tomb is still empty, and Christ is risen? Because the reality is that the world doesn't need another theory, theorem, or proposal, but what the world needs to know is that over 2,000 years ago, there was One who looked over the balconies of heaven, saw our sin-sick situation, came down through 42 generations, came through the womb of a virgin girl, was born in Bethlehem, raised in Nazareth, died on Calvary, three days later was raised from the grave, 50 days after that poured out His Holy Spirit, and one day He is coming back again!

Can Jesus get a witness?

Can Jesus count on you to encourage somebody today that:

- He picked me up, turned me around, He placed my feet on solid ground!
- He healed my body. He saved my soul.
- He made me stronger in my broken places.
- He turned my mourning into dancing. He turned my sackcloth into gladness.
- He took my latter days and made them better than my past.
- He's food on my table, clothes on my back, a friend when I'm friendless, a shelter in the time of storms!

Can Jesus get a witness?

Our text for consideration is found in the gospel written by the Apostle Matthew. Matthew was written 8-15 years post-resurrection, and is the only gospel to use the Greek word *ekklesia* or church. Forty-three percent of this book is devoted to Jesus's teaching—the most out of all four of the gospels. In Matthew's gospel we gain insight into the concerns of Matthew's church just a few years after Jesus died. It's as if Matthew handed us a telescope to view the experiences of Christians in his day to show us how they apply to the church of today. In the chapter we're looking at, chapter 28, it is Sunday morning—the day after the Jewish Sabbath. Verse one records that the original 'Mary, Mary' (Mary Magdalene and the other Mary), have returned on the morning of the third day to visit the tomb where the body of their crucified Savior lay. However, an angel at the tomb reports to them in verse 6 that, "He is not here; for He is risen, as He has said."

After this, Mary-Mary followed the angel's instructions, put their track shoes on, and ran to share the good news with the waiting disciples. Lo and behold, they ran into the post-resurrection, pre-ascension Jesus Himself. However, verse 11 is where the narrative takes a crazy twist. We find here that not everybody is happy about Jesus being risen. In fact, some of the religious leaders, perhaps out of fear of embarrassment and shame by their community that Jesus' words have come true, have gathered together and paid Roman soldiers to spread the lie from the pit of hell that Jesus' disciples had stolen His body from the tomb while everyone was asleep. And sadly, Matthew records in verse 15 that some of the Jews, more than 8 years after this lie was told, were STILL believing it!

Let me pause right here and say to you; when folks are telling you things, you'd better consider the source before you believe them. You can't believe everything you hear about someone. There are people at your job, and even at church, who don't care about propelling the truth; all they care about is perpetuating a lie. So ALWAYS consider the source!

Nonetheless, the Bible says that the 11 disciples (they were minus the betrayer, Judas Iscariot) proceeded to Galilee up the mountain that Jesus had designated. Isn't it amazing how in the lowest moments of our lives, God will occasion an elevated place for us to prepare our lives to be repositioned? And I want to encourage somebody: If, like Jesus' disciples, you are coming out of one of the worst experiences of your life, I dare you to keep marching up to that place where Jesus said He will meet you. When you get there, you'll find that God will give you all the voice and vision you need to have victory in your valley. That's why just a few chapters earlier, in Matthew chapter 5, right after the selection of the disciples in chapter 4, Jesus sat them all down on the side of a mountain and began to teach them what they would need for the rest of their lives. And, if we're serious about the call that God has on our lives, we have to get to the place where we are willing to turn off *Housewives of Atlanta*, disconnect from Facebook for a minute, and press into an elevated place with God. We must say, like the prophet Habakkuk, that, "I will stand upon my watch, and set me upon the tower, and will watch to see what he will say unto me, and what I shall answer when I am reproved" (Habakkuk 2:1).

Even Moses found out, after encountering God in a burning but unconsumed bush, that sometimes in your lowest moments, He will send you to an elevated place to hear from Him in an unusual way. Because if God can change your perspective, then He can propel you toward your purpose.

There ought to be SOMEBODY reading this that can testify that:
I was down and out...
I thought I wasn't going to make it...
I had more adversity than accomplishments...
more burdens than blessings...
more challenges than championships...
more devastation than destiny...
more evil than excellence...
more failure than fortitude...

BUT GOD! God invited me to an elevated place. He picked me up. He dusted me off. I began to see my situation for what it really was. Take example from the hymn by Cleavant Derricks:

Now let us have a little talk with Jesus,
Let us tell Him all about our troubles,
He will hear our faintest cry,
And He will answer by-and-by.

Now when you feel a little prayer wheel turning,
And you know a little fire is burning,
You will find a little talk with Jesus makes it right.

"Yes, that little talk with Jesus will make it right!"

Sometimes God will occasion an elevated place for you to experience Him in an unusual way. As we consider how to be an effective witness for Jesus Christ, I want to examine 3 things:

1. The Authority of a Witness
2. The Assignment of a Witness
3. The Assurance of a Witness

1. The authority of a witness

In verse 18, Jesus says that if you're going to be an effective witness for Him, you need to know the authority of a witness. In other words, you need to know **why** you can go do what He has told you to do. Watch the text. In verse 18 Jesus says specifically, "All power is given unto me in heaven and in earth." I wondered why Jesus would first address His disciples concerning His authority. Then I backed up and took a look at verse 17. The Bible says that some worshipped, BUT SOME doubted.

Perhaps a similar sentiment has transported itself from a mountainside in Galilee to a living room, coffee shop, park, or wherever you are reading this right now. Because I know that even as holy hands are lifted, while we worship God, somebody is doubting whether they are called, capable, and competent enough to spread the gospel in what seems to be enemy territory. Somebody may even be asking himself or herself, "With all the hell that's breaking loose in our world, what authority do I have to go tell people about Jesus? I haven't been to theological school. I don't know the Bible like that. I'm shy. I like to work by myself."

Well, baby, I have some Good News for you! You can go forward because God has given you the authority to do with Him what you cannot do by yourself. You see, when you go, you go in the authority of the God of Abraham, Isaac, and Jacob! When you go, you go in the authority of the One who spoke the cosmos into creation. You go in the authority of the One who has been here since before been here got here!

That's why when Moses, in his insecurity, asked God, "God, when I go before Pharaoh, who do I say sent me?" God answered simply, "Tweet that wretched king and tell him 'I AM' sent you."

You know that anybody who can go by the title "I AM" must be someone not to be reckoned with. That's who is on your side. Right now, I wish you'd be honest with yourself and say,

"Self, there are areas where I have lost my God-ordained authority. I've lost my authority in my home. I've lost my authority over my body. Over my educational dreams. I've lost authority in my thought life. I try to stay focused, but before I know it, I'm sitting in church but my mind is at the club. God help me, I've lost my authority!"

Have you ever taken something to a pawn shop? You sell your stuff in a time of desperation. But then, when you get your financial authority back, you go back to the shop and get your stuff. I'm telling you: get your spiritual stuff back! Get your spiritual authority back.

I dare you to be serious enough about your witness to grab your neighbor by the hand, look them in the eye and tell them, "We're coming out of this thing! There are too many souls that need to be saved. I'm tired of feeling insecure. I'm tired of feeling 'less than.' By God we are going into the devil's territory. We're knocking on the door of hell and telling the devil, 'Give me my authority! Jesus gave it to me and I want it back!'"

Close your eyes. Count to three, and visualize pulling your neighbor out of the pit of hell. PULL! Get your authority back. Don't get so caught up in your terrestrial doubts that you forget about your celestial authority. The authority of the witness says you can go in the name of Jesus because He doesn't have some of the power, He has ALL of the power!

2. The assignment of a witness

Jesus Christ shows us the authority of His witnesses, but He also gives an assignment to His witness. He gives a mission. Look at verses 19 and 20. Jesus says the assignment, the mission, the goal is to "Go, teach, baptize, and teach some more." I hear a lot of people talk about the "baptize" and "teach" parts of this mission, but I don't hear a lot about the "go" part. If you are an aficionado of the Greek language you'll know that the word "go" in Greek is *poreuomai* and it occurs 157 times in the King James Version of the Bible. Every time it's used,

3 - Don't Be Bitter, Be Better

"And when Joseph's brethren saw that their father was dead, they said, Joseph will peradventure hate us, and will certainly requite us all the evil which we did unto him. And they sent a messenger unto Joseph, saying, They father did command before he died, saying, So shall ye say unto Joseph, Forgive, I pray thee now, the trespass of thy brethren, and their sin; for they did unto thee evil: and now, we pray thee, forgive the trespass of the servants of the God of thy father. And Joseph wept when they spake unto him. And his brethren also went and fell down before his face; and they said, Behold, we be thy servants. And Joseph said unto them, Fear not: for am I in the place of God? But as for you, ye thought evil against me; but God meant it unto good, to bring to pass, as it is this day, to save much people alive."

Genesis 50:15-20

A LEMON, BY nature, is tart and bitter to the taste. However, if you squeeze the juice of a lemon into water and stir in some sugar, you will find that the lemon that once was bitter has become much better.

Likewise, cough syrup—old school cough syrup, that is—is downright nasty and bitter. However, if you chase the cough syrup with a drink of orange juice, you'll find that the medicine that was once bitter has become better.

Do you remember those great big ice cream truck pickles? They are sour with a capital S! But I found out that if you stick a peppermint stick in the middle of that pickle and wait a little while, you'll find that what was once sour and bitter has become better.

As we examine life's sour lemons, life's nasty cough syrups, and life's bitter pickles, the question arises, "How do you deal when your ability to cope has collapsed?"

I believe there is somebody reading this who is not too proud to say, "Preacher, I'm doing the best I can here to keep it together, but the truth is, deep down on the inside, there is a level of bitterness that I am wrestling with. I'm bitter because:

- It seems like I've experienced my share of adversity, but not accomplishments.
- It seems like I have more burdens than blessings.
- I've had more challenges than championships.
- I'm depressed, instead of walking in my destiny.
- More doors seem to be closed than open.
- I'm a good woman and I deserve a good man.
- I'm a good man and I deserve a good woman.
- It seems I stay sick and tired and tired and sick.
- And Lord, I've got to be honest... times are tart... the situation is sour... my 'right now' is nasty... and Lord, I'm bitter!"

Well, beloved, the good news for you is that God gave you the same power and ability that He gave to Adam and Eve in the Garden of Eden—the ability to make a decision. I've been sent on a divine assignment to let you know that today is the day, this is the place, and now is the time for you to make a power move in your life. It is time for you to decide that:

- You really are more than a conqueror through Christ Jesus.
- Greater is He who is in you than He who is in the world.
- You might be pressed, but you won't be crushed.
- You might be persecuted, but you won't be abandoned.
- You might be struck down, but you will not be destroyed.

You see, the power of your testimony will be directly affected by how you decide to go through the most challenging moments of your life. You've got to decide, like the hymn writer of old that, YES:

The road is rough,
The going gets tough,
and sometimes the hills are hard to climb.
But I started out a long time ago,
There's no doubt in my mind,
I have decided to make Jesus my choice.

If you don't remember anything else from this chapter, I want you to know that you don't have to be bitter; you can be better.

Thread throughout the tapestry of the text in Genesis is the concept of beginnings. Not only is Genesis the very first book of the Bible, it records the genesis (or beginning) of all of God's creation, and it records the commencement of God's work among His chosen people. In Genesis 50:15-20, we examine one of the most complex characters in canonicity in the person of Joseph.

You likely know Joseph's story. His progression from dream-interpreting shepherd to minister of Egypt is described by one scholar as one of the more layered and elaborate stories in the Hebrew Bible. Joseph's life is a series of highs and lows—both literally and figuratively. After being the favored son of his father, Jacob, and bragging about a dream he had in which he was set as ruler over his 11 other brothers, the brothers decide to throw him into a pit. They take it a step further and sell him into slavery. Later, Joseph finds favor with Potiphar, a high officer of Pharaoh's. Joseph is put in charge over all of Potiphar's household and things go well for him, until he is imprisoned on trumped up rape charges after refusing Potiphar's wife's sexual advances. Further along in Joseph's story, he rises to a position of prominence once again. He conceals his identity when his brothers come to him for help during a famine. He tests the brothers by locking up his brother Simeon until the rest of them go and get his youngest brother, Benjamin (Genesis 42:33-34). Twenty years had gone by since the brothers had sold Joseph into slavery. Their father, Jacob, is reluctant to let Benjamin go. After all, Benjamin was the last child Jacob had from his wife Rachael. But he has no choice and once all of them are standing before Joseph, Joseph reveals his identity.

In Joseph's response to his brothers' plea for forgiveness, we see the story take a strange twist.

You would expect someone who was thrown into a pit to be bitter—but Joseph was not.

You would expect someone who had been sold into slavery to be bitter—but Joseph was not.

You would expect that someone who had been falsely imprisoned and wrongly accused of rape to be bitter—but Joseph was not.

Joseph's response shows us that we don't have to be bitter, we can make an informed decision to be better. I want to examine 3 aspects of Joseph's response to his conspirators, a.k.a. his brothers, in verse 20. We will examine:

1. The Reality of Joseph's Situation
2. The Rationale in Joseph's Situation
3. The Redemption in Joseph's Situation

1. The reality of Joseph's situation

As we examine the reality of Joseph's situation, we recognize the fact of life that there will be times when people are going to plot evil against you. You've got to face the reality that there will be people who don't mean you any good. Watch the text; Joseph (in my own paraphrase of verse 20) says to his brothers, "You thought evil against me. And you didn't just try to harm me—you tried to take a brotha' out completely!"

The Hebrew word for "thought" in verse 20 means to weave or fabricate something. The Hebrew word for "evil" means adversity or calamity. We see that Joseph has apparently faced the reality that the people closest to him tried to kill him. Genesis 37:4 reads, "When his brothers saw that their father loved him (Joseph) more than any of them, they hated him and could not speak a kind word to him."

Listen to me, friend, you need to know that if you can get over the shock of WHO it was that hurt you, then you can begin to heal! You need to face the reality that sometimes the closest people to you will try and take you out!

- Sometimes, people pat you on the back because they're trying to find a soft spot to stab you.
- Sometimes, people will pull a Julius Caesar on you, leaving you asking, "Et tu, Brute?"

And hear this: the enemy is not always an outside enemy. Sometimes the person trying to take you out is the inner-me. Reality is that some things are not your fault, but they are your problem, and you won't move forward, you won't advance, you won't progress, until you reach way down inside, throw your head back, and ask God to help you get over it! Some folks are what they are—they don't mean you any good—but you can't let that stop you from doing what God called you to do. In Jesus' name, GET OVER IT!

I love watching the Olympic games. Discus, shot-put, basketball, tennis, relays—they are all exciting. I've talked to some Olympic athletes and although they all train hard, many have the most respect for the athletes who run the 300 meter hurdles. Not only do these athletes have to run fast, but every few steps they have to jump over an obstacle. Let me tell you, not only do you need to train to run this Christian race, but you need to train to GET OVER the obstacles. I can hear the hymnologist of old saying:

Trouble in my way, I've had to cry sometime, I lay awake at night, but that's alright, cause Jesus will fix it after awhile.

The reality of Joseph's situation shows us that people will plot evil against you, but, in the name of Jesus, you have the power to get over it!

2. The rationale in Joseph's situation

Not only do we gain strength to be better from the reality of Joseph's situation, but we are also encouraged by the rationale Joseph uses in his situation. Look at verse 20. The Bible says, "Ye thought evil against me, but God meant it unto good."

Joseph uses the same Hebrew word for the word "meant" that he used to describe what his brothers "thought." That is to say that Joseph recognized that God's presence in his situation drew positive purpose out of his brothers' evil plot. Beloved, you need to know today that God can take the same thing that the enemy tried to use to harm you and use it instead to help you! Look at what Joseph says: "BUT God!" If you know the king's English, you'll recognize that the word "but" used is a coordinating conjunction. In the English language there are 7 of these conjunctions:

1. "for" explains a reason
2. "and" adds one thing to another
3. "nor" shows an alternate circumstance
4. "or" presents a choice
5. "yet" introduces a logical idea
6. "so" indicates a consequence

However, "but" shows contrast. I dare you to take a look back over your life; take a trip down memory lane. I bet you won't get far before you have to stop and thank God for His divine intervention. Can you thank God for showing you the contrast of how it turned out versus how bad it could have been?

The story is told of the violinist Paganini who, during a performance, broke all of his strings except for one. Holding up his violin to the crowd, he said, "Ladies and gentlemen, one string and Paganini."

Sometimes, you just need to go to a secret place in your mind and have a woman to woman or a man to man talk with your difficulties and say, "You almost took me out, I was down for the count, I almost threw in the towel, BUT I've got one string left. As long as I got one string left, I can keep on playing."

All I'm trying to tell you is when you realize that God is all you have, then you find out that God is all you need. Joseph said:

I should have been killed by my brothers... BUT GOD...
I should have died in the pit... BUT GOD...
I should have died in slavery... BUT GOD...
I should have still been in jail on false charges... BUT GOD...

Find someone in your life today who you can grab by the hand, look in the eye and say, "I don't have time to tell you my whole story, so I'll sum it up like this... BUT GOD!"

My testimony is that I...
... never should have made it, BUT GOD!
... never could have made it, BUT GOD!
... don't know how I'm gonna make it, BUT GOD!
... have a marriage that is on the rocks, BUT GOD!
... seem like I can't get well, my body is sick, BUT GOD!
... am benefiting from divine intervention!

My rationale dictates that God's presence will draw positive purpose out of the enemy's evil plot!

3. The redemption in Joseph's situation

On this journey to be better, not bitter, we've seen Joseph's reality and we've witnessed Joseph's rationale. In the final portion of Joseph's response, we see the redemption in Joseph's situation. The text reads that Joseph recognized that everything he had to go through was necessary so that many lives could be saved. I don't know about you, but I am so glad my pain is not without purpose. I'm so glad my test is not without a testimony. I'm so glad that my challenge is not without a championship.

You need to know today that your shout is not that God gave you a new house after what you went through. (Even though I like new houses.) Your shout is not that God gave you a new spouse. (Even though I like weddings.) Your shout is that God has a redemptive purpose through your pain. The shout is that even though your problems were, and maybe still are, great, greater is He who is in you than he who is in the world.

Is there anybody reading this who knows we serve a great God? He is so great that He's more concerned with your development than your deliverance. He's so great that He woke you up this morning and started you on your way. He's so great that when nothing else could help, love was still able to lift you.

I'm reminded of a conversation I had with a retired Brigadier General, who was an F-105 Thunderchief pilot in Vietnam. During that time, his plane was shot down and he spent 63 months in a POW camp known as the Hanoi Hilton. This general told me, "Fighter pilots are known for being obnoxious, arrogant guys who are trained to step into the cockpit of a million dollar weapons system and pride themselves by winning fights in the air. However, strip a fighter pilot down to his boxers and place him in the clutches of a POW camp, taking away everything but his will to survive, then you will see the real fight in him."

My brother or sister, you might be stripped down, bearing the nakedness of your emotions. Circumstances might make you feel like you are sucking life's lemons, drinking nasty cough syrup, and eating a sour pickle all at the same time. But you don't have to be bitter. Beloved, you can choose to be better. I am so glad that I don't have to lean on your example, and you don't have to lean on my example. Together we can lean on the One who left us the ultimate example of how not to be bitter, but to be better.

Closing prayer:

Thank You, God that in every circumstance I have the chance to show Your mighty power in my life. God, let me draw on You so when life is hard, and in the difficulties I face, those around me would not see me as bitter, but I take every chance to show the world that I am better because of Who I belong to. Give me the wisdom and resolve that You gave to Joseph all those years ago. Let me always remember that You are greater than any enemy that will come up against me. Amen.

fall on people and wonder:

- What is it that makes people run when ain't nobody chasin' 'em?
- What is it that makes people laugh when ain't nothin' funny?
- What is it that makes the old deacons squall when everybody else is quiet?

Then I got a little bit older and I discovered that feeling the weight of God's presence is enough for all of those things. The first thing you need to do, though, is get God's presence off of the cart and get it back in your hands. View God's presence from the proper perspective!

2. Privileges

David shows us in this narrative that when God's presence makes the difference in your life, it benefits you to view God's presence from the proper perspective. But, when you trust that God's presence makes the difference, you also know that God's presence in your life has its privileges. Have a look at verse 11. The Bible says, "And the ark of the LORD continued in the house of Obededom the Gittite three months: and the LORD blessed Obededom, and all his household."

I need to explain something about this fella here named Obededom. Biblical scholars tend to agree that Obededom was most likely not connected to Israel and the household of faith. This brotha' never got the perfect attendance award for going to church. He was most likely a Philistine who was a protected alien. Ancient historian Josephus also notes that Obededom was a poor man. However, during the three months that the presence of God resided at his house, he emerged out of poverty. In fact, the Bible says that Obededom and, not *some*, but his *entire* household was blessed. They got blessed just for being in the house! And I know that's a good word for somebody reading this. You can be blessed just by being in the house.

Take a minute to reflect. You know there have been times that you got blessed from being in God's house:

- You used to open the club and shut it down, but if you did nothing else, you found yourself on Sunday morning in God's house (hangover and all) and God gave you a word that blessed you.

- You used to stay overnight somewhere you shouldn't on Saturday night, but you always had church clothes with you. God blessed you to stop straddling the spiritual fence, all because you kept coming to His house.
- Your marriage was on the rocks. One of you was going to take the blender and the other claimed the toaster, and the kids were acting like they lost their everlasting minds. But you kept coming to God's house and He blessed you.
- You didn't know how you were ever going to graduate with those test scores. You didn't know how you were going to make it when Daddy walked out or when Mama left. But you kept coming to God's house and God blessed you!

Everything you need can be found in God's house: Love, joy, peace, patience, kindness, goodness, faithfulness, gentleness, and self-control.

I don't want to take it for granted that everybody reading this is on the victorious side of their testimony, so I've got to explain what this word "blessed" is all about. The Hebrew word for "blessed" is *barak*. This work literally means to kneel down and bless. Please listen, child of God, God told me to tell you that if you find yourself struggling with the issues of life, just keep your presence in His presence because if you keep coming and participating at the house, God will kneel down and barak your world. Perhaps you need to take a moment right now and be your own self-help group and make the bold declaration that, "I need God to barak my world! I'm declaring a moratorium on my tears. Lord, barak that! I need you to bless it!"

Sickness? God, barak that!
Depression? God, barak that!
Recession? God barak that!
Unemployment? God barak that!
Low self-esteem? God, barak that!

If what you need blessed is too much for you to even utter the words, just ask, "God, barak it."

Sometimes you have to say, "God, I heard about how you turned a cosmic chaos into a masterpiece. Do it for me. I heard that you stopped the sun so Joshua could get his work done. Do it for me. I heard how Moses lifted his staff and split the Red Sea. Do it for me!"

God's presence has its privileges.

3. Personal praise

God shows us through David's real life story that we must view God from the proper perspective and that, as a child of God, His presence has its privileges. Finally, this text shows us that God's presence in your life ought to initiate a personal praise. God's presence will kick off a praise in you that has some personality wrapped up in it!

In verse 5 of 2 Samuel 6, we read that David and Israel played instruments before the Lord. This was before David truly understood how to handle God's presence. Afterward, when David had proper perspective and he saw firsthand how God's presence had barak'ed Obededom's world, verse 14 records that David went from *playing* to *dancing*! David went from commemorating the event with everyone else to celebrating the experience all by himself.

Up to this point in the Bible, no men had been recorded as dancing before the Lord. In fact, in David's day, some people may have raised their eyebrows at his sexuality because he danced. But David didn't care. It wasn't *their* praise, it was *his* praise! David was determined that he was going to praise God, even if he had to praise by himself! When you understand that God still allows His presence in your life after you've left Him so many times, that's enough to make you praise the Lord in a personal kind of way.

Can Jesus get a witness that isn't afraid to praise God in a personal way?

For every mountain He's brought me over, for every trial He's seen me through, for every blessing, Hallelujah!

For breath in my body, for the food on my table, for the clothes on my back, for the family who loves me, for blessings yet unseen, Hallelujah!

Call on Him! Give Him glory! If you know Him, you ought to lift Him! Go tell someone today that, "God's presence makes the difference!"

Closing Prayer:

Holy Spirit, Thank You for reminding me that God's presence makes all the difference. I don't want to go through the motions, I want to praise with power. I want to personally praise the LORD in all things, no matter who is looking. I pray that I will not be afraid to bear the weight of God's presence. Amen.

5 - Praise in the Middle of a Blackout

"Yea, though I walk through the valley of the shadow of death, I will fear no evil: for thou art with me; thy rod and thy staff they comfort me."

Psalm 23:4

I REALLY ENJOY keeping up with pop culture. Recently, I stumbled upon an article about British pop music star Jessie J. In the article, the reporter asked Jessie to recall how she felt during an event called Black Out. Initially hesitant to rehash what happened, Jessie J conceded and shared the details of that unforgettable night.

Back in 2011, Jessie J participated in a music festival called Black Out. All of the artists agreed to sing in total darkness. She didn't think much about what those conditions would be like, Jessie J simply agreed to be in the show and prepared her songs. On the night of the show, things took a horrible turn for her.

As soon as she stepped on the stage, she suffered a panic attack. Her hands began to sweat, her breathing accelerated, her blood pressure elevated, and above all, she thought she was going to die. Even though she knew why it was dark and she knew what was going on, she suffered from anxiety and it got the best of her that night. The reporter asked if Jessie finished the show and she shared that she did not. She admitted to begging and pleading for the lights to be turned on, but her request was not fulfilled, forcing her to exit the stage.

You might be wondering, "What does this have to do with me? I'm not a pop star. I don't get paid to perform. I'm an everyday person. I'm a mother, father, retiree, grandparent, student—but not a pop star."

Well, child of God, I do believe that each of us has had a Jessie J experience. Someone, like Jessie, is standing on this stage called "life," ready to sing your song and do your dance. However, when the moment comes, you have a full blown panic attack. The lights are off, your palms are sweating, your heart rate is accelerating, your blood pressure is going up, and to top it all off, your pleading seems to fall on deaf ears. You are in a blackout. Your marriage is falling apart. Your children are acting strange. The doctor has given you a devastating diagnosis. You're failing your classes. You don't know if you are coming or going. You may be pleading with God, "Father! Turn on the lights! Call the energy company! Plug in a night light because Lord, I need to see You!"

You might feel that God doesn't see you tripping over your feet, confused, stumbling, and trying to find your way. Hear this, beloved: The Lord hears your request. What you have to realize is that, when the lights are off, you must trust Him, even when you cannot trace Him.

You can still praise God in the middle of your blacked out situation!

As we take a look at the book of Psalms as a whole, we find it is a collection of songs written in response to events happening in everyday people's lives. Entire communities would sing them in unison during times of worship. Most of the psalms were written to be sung with others during corporate worship. You see, there is power in corporate worship because your neighbor may have something you need, and you may have something your neighbor needs.

The book of Psalms can be divided into five books. One author notes that the book of Psalms in its totality has a two-fold operation: First, individually the psalms explore an honest spiritual response to God, and second, the entire book of Psalms celebrates God's work in the history of His people.

And it is here in our text, Psalm 23, we see that David is having an honest conversation with God. When was the last time you had an open and honest conversation with your God? When was the last time you said, "Lord, I need thee, O, I need thee; Every hour I need thee; O bless me now, my Savior, I come to thee." When was the last time you asked God, "Pass me not, O gentle Savior.

Hear my humble cry; While on others Thou art calling, Do not pass me by."

This psalm is unlike any other that David has written. One scholar noted that many of David's psalms are laments, but the 23rd Psalm is filled with expression of delight in God's great goodness and dependability. David likens himself to a sheep, and his shepherd is God. From his past experience, David was quite familiar with the shepherd/sheep relationship. As a real-life shepherd, he knew the attention, care, and kindness that a shepherd provided to all of his sheep, and acknowledged that if he was to follow, he would have to render himself as a sheep: quiet, meek, sociable, and silent at the hands of the shepherd.

In the very first verse David writes, "The Lord is my shepherd; I shall not want." He acknowledges God as his provider.

In verse 2 he continues, "He maketh me to lie down in green pastures: he leadeth me beside the still waters." Here he notes that God is a caregiver.

Verse 3: "He restoreth my soul: he leadeth me in the paths of righteousness for his name's sake." David recognizes God as his restorer.

And then, in verse 4, David shows us three reasons why we can have a praise in the midst of a blackout.

1. Darkness will come

Verse 4 begins, "Yea, though I walk through the valley of the shadow of death." Geographically speaking, a valley is a low area situated between hills or mountains, typically with a river or stream flowing through it. You have to have been at a place of elevation before entering the valley. Likewise, to get to the mountaintop (a place of high elevation), you have to go through a valley. Your time in the valley is not an accident, but a part of God's plan! We do not serve an accidental God.

Romans 8:28 reads, "And we know that all things work together for good to them that love God, to them who are called according to his purpose." God does this for a purpose! And if that doesn't encourage you, then maybe realizing that David tells us, "Yea, though I *walk*..." Walk! You don't have to run, you don't have to catch a cab, you don't even have to power walk. Take your time and trust that God has a plan for the valley you are going through. Yes, it may be uncomfortable. Yes, you may be ready for it to be over. But trust that God is calling you to come out of it better than when you entered it because your mountaintop is on the way!

While living in Grand Rapids, Michigan, I worked with preschool children and one of the songs we sang frequently was about going on a bear hunt. In the song, children come up against different obstacles in the forest, such as trees, caves, hills, etc. Every time they come to an item, they ask, "What do we do?" After going through a litany of questions, they come to the conclusion, "We can't go over it, we can't go around it, we have to go through it!" Although entertaining for children, this simple song speaks to your life today.

You can't go over it.
You can't go around it.
You have to go through it!

You can face your valley of the shadow of death because you know valleys are meant to be traveled "through."

"The valley of the shadow of death" is translated in Greek as the word for "grave" or, figuratively, "calamity." If we insert this figurative word into the scripture, it reads, "Yea, though I walk through the valley of calamity..." Even in the midst of turmoil, evil, and confusion, you don't have to worry about the outcome because you know God's got your back. Though weapons may form, they will not prosper. Though a valley experience comes, it won't take you out because the God of the mountaintop is the same God in the valley of the shadow of death. Take a minute to look over your life and think of some of the valleys you have had to walk through.

You were told that you were going to lose your job, but you stayed and was able to retire.

You were told that you have a terminal illness, but several years later, you're still here.

You were even told that because your daddy was a nobody and your mama was a nobody, you wouldn't amount to anything, but look at you now, you are educated, prosperous, and living the

6 - God Will Work it Out

"And we know that all things work together for good to them that love God, to them who are called according to his purpose."

Romans 8:28

PASTOR H.B. CHARLES, JR. tells the story of a man who woke up to find himself spitting out water, laying on a sandy shore, wondering where he was. He had been the lone survivor of a terrible shipwreck, and it seemed no help was in sight. It wasn't long before survival instincts interrupted his pity party and he made himself a hut, a shelter, to protect him from the blazing sun. After making the hut, he trekked into a treed area to find food. However, when he returned from his hunt, his hut was engulfed in flames. In despair, he fell to his knees on the shore.

Soon, he saw a ship coming toward the island. It was a rescue! When a crewman reached the shore, the shipwrecked man asked, "How did you find me?"

The crewman replied, "We found you by the smoke signal you sent up."

The shipwrecked man discovered in that moment what the Bible says is true. ALL things really do work together for our good. I've been sent on divine assignment to encourage somebody whose hut is burning. You may be reading this and thinking, "This word ain't for me!" Well, before you skip over it and go to the next message, let me ask you to keep reading because you never know what tomorrow will bring. This chapter is meant to encourage somebody whose hut is burning. Somebody who:

- Is praying for God to put some elastic on their paycheck to make it stretch from one week to the next.

- Has had to stare into a grave as deep as love and as long as life.
- Is struggling with the tension between God's proclamation and His demonstration, and isn't sure that God will do what He said He would do.

I don't know about you, but every once in a while, when life gets really heavy, and when what I imagined doesn't look at all like what I see, I sometimes reach my Popeye point. Remember the beefy sailor from the cartoon? He'd reach his breaking point and cry out, "I've had all I can takes and I can't takes no more!" I, too, reach my Popeye point. And in that moment, when I "can't takes no more!" God encourages, chastises, and reminds me that despite my circumstances and despite what it looks like or feels like, He will work it out. You see, I found that the real question we have to ask ourselves is, "Do I have FAITH that God will do what He said He would do?" Do you believe God can do His thing in your life?

You need to know that it takes faith to believe that which you can't see with your natural eyes will supernaturally appear. It takes faith to believe that it's coming together when it seems like it is falling apart. You know what faith is, don't you?

- The writer of Hebrews said faith is the substance of things hoped for, and the evidence of things not seen.
- Theologian C.H. Spurgeon said, "A little faith will bring your soul to heaven; a great faith will bring heaven to your soul."
- Faith is what allows you to see the invisible, believe the incredible, and receive the impossible.
- Faith allows you to do without the indispensable and bear the intolerable.
- Faith is not believing that God can, but knowing that God will!

And is there anybody reading this who knows that sometimes you've gotta see it before you see it, so you can know what IT is when you see it? YOU know that faith gives you glasses to see in the supernatural what you can't see in the natural. Faith will help you see that weeping may endure for the night, but JOY comes in the morning! Faith helps you see that you are pressed, but NOT crushed. You are perplexed, but NOT driven to despair.

And if you don't remember anything else from this message, I

3. There is synergy in your circumstances

When you know God will work it out, Paul encourages you to not only be sure of your soul salvation and to see God's sovereignty in your circumstances, but the remainder of verse 28 shows that there is supernatural cooperation among the issues of life. There is synergy in your circumstances.

Verse 28 reads, "all things *work together*..." Together! The Greek word *sunergeo* means to be a fellow worker with, to cooperate with. It's the word from which we get our English word "synergy." A modern definition of synergy suggests that two or more things are working together to produce a result that neither one could achieve by itself. In essence, when God is the subject, object, and predicate of all you do—when God is in it—stuff has a strange way of working out. Now, it may not work out the way you want it to, but when God is in it, it always works out the way it needs to. Can Jesus get a witness that all things have a divine way of working out in your favor? You just have to see God in it!

I just don't understand:

How He spoke and created the whole world, but I see God in it.

How He took dust and made a man, but I see God in it.

How He stopped the sun so that Joshua could get his work done, but I see God in it.

How Daniel read the writing on the wall, but I see God in it.

How He opened blinded eyes, but I see God in it.

How He dried up the woman's issue of blood, but I see God in it.

How He came to be born through a virgin, but I see God in it.

How He marched up a hill called Calvary, had the strength to go to a gruesome death for my sins, suffered, died, and was buried, but three days later rose from the grave... How He carried my sins far away because in that death HE SAVED ME, but I see God in it!

When I look back over my life and I think things over, I can truly say that I've been blessed. I've cried. I've laid awake at night. I've been through the fire. I've been through the flood. I've been broken in pieces and have seen lightning flashes from above. But through it all, I remember that HE loves me and He cares. He will never put more on me than He knows I can bear.

My testimony is that God will work it out!

Closing Prayer:

God, I claim Your promises today. I know You have saved my soul. I know You are sovereign. I know You work it all out for my good, even when I don't see it. I love You and I raise my hands high in holy praise to You in each circumstance I face. Amen and amen!

connection. In verse 3, all David wants to know is if there is anyone left to whom he can fulfill his promise. Ziba answers the question, then takes the time to point out Mephibosheth's condition—almost as if his physical condition would be a barrier or prohibit the king's kindness. What Ziba didn't know was that the favor David planned to show had nothing to do with this crippled man's condition; this kindness had everything to do with his connection to the king! I don't know about you, but I am so glad that my connection is not related to my condition and that the King continues to show me a kindness that I don't deserve!

When Kan'Dace and I were newly married, we had newly married bills to pay. I have to confess, when you have just enough money to pay a big bill, a small bill becomes a small priority. One day, a friend called to invite me to lunch. I didn't get to talk to him, but someone DID answer my phone. It was an automated voice that said, "At the subscriber's request, this phone cannot accept any phone calls." You see, because of the condition of my bank account, I didn't pay my phone bill, and I was consequently disconnected.

I thank God that His kingdom operates on abundance and that God doesn't have to manage His heavenly resources the way you and I have to manage our earthly ones. We are the benefactors of a Savior who paid the ultimate cost to get us and keep us connected, even when our condition declared that we didn't deserve it. And now we sing our testimony in unison with the hymnologist of old:

I hear the Savior say,
"Thy strength indeed is small;
Child of weakness, watch and pray,
Find in Me thine all in all."

Jesus paid it all,
All to Him I owe;
Sin had left a crimson stain,
He washed it white as snow.

Is there someone in your life who needs to hear, "Don't you throw in the towel! Jesus saw your condition and He washed it white as snow and you are still connected!"? If so, call them, text, them, Facebook, or e-mail them and let them know. The King is showing you a kindness that you don't deserve!

2. Restoration

This text teaches us that not only will God show us unmerited favor, but He'll also "do" within us a unique restoration. God will restore you. Merriam-Webster defines restoration as "the act of bringing something back to its former position or condition." However, the Bible shows us that God's restoration won't bring you back to your former condition, God's restoration will leave you *better* than you were before.

In verse 7 David says, "I will restore to you all the land of your grandfather Saul." David gave Mephibosheth ALL of the paternal estate of Saul, thereby restoring to him more than what was legally his. And I believe if you could have asked Mephibosheth he would tell you, "Through the challenges you will face in life, the delay of God's promises does not mean you are being denied. That is grace."

If God promised it, you shall have it because God is a restorer of all that is lost. And if I may prophetically speak life into a dying situation for a moment, let me encourage you that there is a lot of living to do beyond life's broken pieces. Your delay is not your denial and God will restore you.

If you don't believe me, ask Moses. He'll tell you how even though he had physically broken the original covenant stones given to him by God, God told him to, "Cut two tablets of stone like the former ones, and I will write on them the words that were on the former tablets." God did this because He is a restorer of ALL that is lost.

Ask the crying mother in Luke chapter 7, and she'll invite you to her hometown of Nain and tell you how Jesus raised her son, the fruit of her womb, from the dead and literally handed him back to her because He's God like that and He's a restorer of ALL that is lost.

Stand up like the man or woman of God that you are and stop giving up on your family, your dreams, your aspirations, your financial well-being, and whatever else God has ordained in your life. I hear the Spirit of the Lord saying, "Baby, you're pressed, but not crushed. Persecuted, but not abandoned, you might be struck down, but you are not destroyed. Come to me, even if you are in broken pieces because I am a restorer of ALL that is lost!"

God makes all things new. Satan comes to steal, kill, and destroy, but the King came that you might have life and life more abundantly! If the devil had his way, you would be dead. The devil's plans are that you lose your mind, but God is a restorer of ALL that was lost.

Take a moment now and tell Satan, "Whatever you stole, I want it back!"

Peace! I want it back.
Family! I want it back.
Finances! I want it back.
Self-control! I want it back.
Joy! I want it back.
Love! I want it back.
My thoughts! I want them back!

Say it, "Satan, I am taking it all back because God is a restorer of all that was lost!"

3. Change

Not only will God show you kindness that you don't deserve and restore you all that you've lost, but know for a fact that an encounter with the King will permanently change your life. I'm not telling you what I *think*, I'm telling you what I know! In verse 7, David tells Mephibosheth, "You shall eat at my table sometimes."

Hold up! That wasn't it. He said, "You shall eat at my table on special holidays."

Nope. He didn't say that either. David told Mephibosheth, "You shall eat at my table ALWAYS!" David showed this crippled, undeserving man that there is permanent power and privilege associated with an encounter with the king. I bet Mephibosheth would tell us that hanging out at Machir's house was alright, but it was nothing compared to what happened when he received a permanent place in the king's palace. Know this: You may have experienced some nice hangout spots in your life, but there is nothing like the permanent power and privilege you receive from an encounter with the King of Kings!

Let me try and make a plain illustration of this. Many have come to know me as Pastor Fredricc Gerard Brock. However, when I go back to the neighborhood where I grew up, I'm simply known as Fred—Virgil Senior and Janice's baby boy. I must confess, my bloodline, like Mephibosheth's, has been good to me. I'm 6'4", and this body that my kinfolk passed on to me and blessed me with has allowed me to do a lot of things. I've dunked a basketball, I've signed autographs as a professional athlete, and I can even grab those hard-to-reach items on the top shelf! Y'all, my bloodline has been good to me. However, as much as my kinfolk love me, their bloodline can only give me so much. You see, on this journey called life I found that the King's bloodline is the only thing that unequivocally, undisputedly gives me permanent power and privilege.

Through our text study, can Jesus get a witness that He is the ONLY one that can give you permanent power and privilege? God picked you up, turned you around, and places your feet on solid ground! Don't hang out on the premises, stand on the promises. Most of all, forget about simply living the rest of your life, but let your life-changing encounter with the King drive you to live the BEST of your life. Let Him bring you out of Lodebar!

Closing prayer:

Lord Jesus, Thank You for the blood shed on the cross. My faith is in You for grace, restoration, and life-change that will lift me out of Lodebar. Lord, I stand against Satan's schemes to keep me there. You are the war weapon against which no power of the enemy will prevail. I will hold my hands high in praise to You and You alone. Amen.

8 - God Don't Need No Matches

"O LORD, thou hast deceived me, and I was deceived; thou art stronger than I, and hast prevailed: I am in derision daily, every one mocketh me. For since I spake, I cried out, I cried violence and spoil; because the word of the LORD was made a reproach unto me, and a derision, daily. Then I said, I will not make mention of him, nor speak any more in his name. But his word was in mine heart as a burning fire shut up in my bones, and I was weary with forbearing, and I could not stay."

Jeremiah 20:7-9

SOME OF MY fondest teenage memories are the trips I'd make across the country with my daddy in his 18-wheeler. On one particular trip, I remember it was late at night and my daddy was getting tired. We were running low on fuel so my daddy said, "Fred, I'm going to stop at the next truck stop and get some rest because it's late at night, I'm getting tired, and we're running low on fuel."

And, since it was late at night, my daddy was tired, and we were running low on fuel, my daddy did exactly what he said. He pulled into a truck stop, parked the truck, hopped back into the bed, and went to sleep. Strangely though, as low as we were on fuel, he kept the truck running. Listen, I'm not the smartest man in the world, but I've gotta let you in on something. I know why day turns to night (because the earth revolves around the sun), and I know why Daddy got tired (because he had been driving for a long time), but what I could not understand was why, if we were so low on fuel, my daddy would keep the truck running? I believe this message will speak to someone who is driving down this road called life, and for you, it's late at night, your mind, body, and soul are tired, and you're looking at the gas gauge while down on your knees, and it looks like you are running low on fuel. You see, I've been around long enough to know that there are people, problems, and perceptions that can make you experience the darkness, fatigue, and weariness of life. If I had 19 witnesses, I'd make 20 to testify that life can be downright ugly sometimes. Let's be honest:

- You're giving your job the best you've got. You're the first to show up and the last one to leave, but it seems like you are always misunderstood and underappreciated.
- You've studied all night long, you've highlighted till you can't highlight no more, but everybody else keeps making better grades and your parents just don't understand.
- You've given your best in service to the church, you've given your time, talent, and treasure, but frankly, as a Christian, you're tired of being hurt by other Christians; a.k.a. church folks.
- You've loved your family with everything you've got. Your kids may not have everything they want, but you always make sure they have what they need. Yet, when you call on them, they disappear faster than a snowball in the summertime.

And you're left depressed, despondent, and disappointed, asking yourself, "How do I handle the underbelly of life when it's late at night, I'm tired, and I'm running out of fuel?" Well, let me give you this for free, before we see what Jeremiah has to say. My best advice is that you need to know the One who can fan your weary sparks into a flame of hope. You need to know the One who is bigger than any problem you could ever face. You need to know Somebody who is a rater for the underrated, who's an appreciator of the under-appreciated. You need to be in contact with a power, way down deep on the inside of you, who won't allow you to quit this close to the finish line. A supernatural power that will make you give Him the glory for your story. A power that will make you praise Him in the hallway until God opens up the door. As a matter of fact, I like Reverend James Cleveland's resolution when he experienced the night of life, his spirit was tired, and he was running low on fuel. Cleveland said:

I just can't give up now
I've come too far from where I started from
Nobody told me the road would be easy
And I don't believe He brought me this far to leave me.

I want you to know more than anything, now is not the time to give up on the task that God has given you. Now is not the time to give up on your family. Now is not the time to give up on your church. Now is not the time to give up on yourself. If you feel like your fire is going out, remember, God don't need no matches to keep your fire burning 'cause He's fire all by Himself!

As we cut through this text from Jeremiah 20, we find the prophet Jeremiah experiencing a late-at-night, tired, low-fuel situation. We're going to look at:

1. Jeremiah's confrontation
2. Jeremiah's complaint
3. Jeremiah's constraint

Jeremiah is just doing what God told him to do. In chapter 1 of Jeremiah, God had touched Jeremiah's mouth and said, "I have this day set thee over the nations and over the kingdoms, to root out, and to pull down, to destroy, and to throw down, to build, and to plant" (verse 10). Fast forward to chapter 19, God tells Jeremiah to buy a clay potter's jug, take some elders and senior priests with him to the valley of the son of Hinnom. More specifically, God tells Jeremiah to preach a message of destruction, breaking the potter's jug at the potsherd gate as an illustration. Let me tell you something about the potsherd gate. It was literally the city sewage release gate, so you can imagine how it looked and smelled. What I want you to see is that this preacher/prophet was sent with an unfavorable message, to an unfavorable place, and as you can imagine, received an unfavorable response. The Bible says that when Jeremiah came from Topheth (Jer. 19:14) and spoke the Lord's message in the Lord's house, somebody got mad! Let me say that again in case you missed the point: **Jeremiah preached the Lord's message, in the Lord's house, and somebody got mad!** And that brings up the confrontation.

1. Jeremiah's Confrontation

When you say what the Lord says, the way God wants you to say it, there is a strong possibility that somebody will get mad. The reality is that part of what God has called you to is to be the person who preaches a life-transforming word of confrontation; a word that challenges people to reflect on how they're living versus how God wants them to live. Most often, the first reaction to this word is anger. Listen, people will get mad when confronted, but it's part of God's transformational process. People don't mind change; what they mind is changing! When God tells you to tell somebody that something in their house has to change, then people do what people do—they get MAD! Let me encourage you, stop getting mad when other people get mad. It's a part of the process. The Bible says that Pashur, Judah's wicked high priest, heard Jeremiah preaching and he arrested him, whipped him, and humiliated him by hanging him in the stocks all night long. The thing I find crazy about this is that as the high priest and temple administrator, Pashur was supposed to be the chief promoter of the prophet. However, his misunderstanding of God's agenda through God's man led him to be Jeremiah's chief problem. And if I might remind you here: You better be careful about making judgments about that which you haven't even tried to understand. Lord, deliver me from people who don't show up to anything, don't pray for the vision or success of Your church, are not concerned about growing in Christ, but ALWAYS want to judge what's going on and they raise the most hell. You better be careful about verbally whipping and locking up that which you don't understand. You see, the Holy Spirit showed me that the anecdote for judging too quickly is to ask questions more frequently. Ask yourself, "Self, when was the last time we asked, 'Why are they doing that?' as opposed to simply stating, 'They're always doing something unnecessary.'"

"Excuse me, can you explain that to me?" is a much better response than, "I'm not going back there because we never used to do things that way." The Civil Rights Movement shows us that people discriminate, criticize, and demonize that which they don't quite understand. Does it make us better when we discriminate against somebody we have never even had a good conversation with? No, it does not. I'll say it again: You better be careful locking up what you don't understand. Jeremiah's confrontation gives us the guarantee that when you preach and live out God's message, somebody will get mad.

2. Jeremiah's Complaint

After Jeremiah is whipped and released from lock-up, he continued to preach God's word. The text then takes a strange twist.

Jeremiah moves from proclaiming to complaining. Jeremiah cries out to God in this dramatic monologue:

- God, I've traveled miles and miles away from home to serve notice to Your people, and I've been nothing but whipped and humiliated!
- Lord, I want to preach Your message, but right now, nobody wants to hear what You've told me to say!
- Lord, I am so fed up, I wish I'd never been born!

In Jeremiah's complaint, we find an action that resonates with an element of the human condition. The reality is that there are times when all you can do is be honest about how ugly and unpleasant it is right now. The late, great Bishop William C. Abney said, "I won't complain," and THAT'S my favorite song of all time. However, some of us got the Bishop's sentiment twisted. He said, "I won't complain." He didn't say, "It's wrong to complain." Nowhere in the Bible does it say that it is wrong to be honest and express dissatisfaction about your current situation. I know this might challenge your theology, but it's right there in the Bible and should not be confused with Paul's message that we are not to grumble. Grumbling over nothing is different from expressing grief over an unpleasant situation. In fact, the majority of the psalms are psalms of lament; psalms in which God's people are simply being honest about the ugly situation they find themselves in. The psalmists say things like:

- How long shall I take counsel in my soul, having sorrow in my heart daily? How long shall mine enemy be exalted over me? (Psalm 13:2)
- O God, how long shall the adversary reproach? (Psalm 74:10)

You see, the first step in solving a problem is to realize that you have one. I've found out that the problem many of us have is that we're too afraid to acknowledge that we are real-life people with real-life issues, so we live our lives addressing the symptoms instead of addressing the real problem. You see, the problem is not in your complaining, the problem comes when all you do is complain, like you are unable to do anything else. But, child of the Most-High God, when your burden is too heavy to bear, when your heart is overwhelmed, you need to be led to a Rock higher than yourself. You need to cry out like the hymnologist of old:

I need thee, oh I need thee,
Every hour I need thee,
Oh bless me now, my Savior
I come to thee

You will never get to the source of the real problem if you don't first keep it real with yourself. I know it hurts, but you will die the way you are if you don't keep it real. When you keep it real, you aren't ashamed to say:

- God, I really am depressed and I need professional help.
- God, I can't leave the pornographic material alone and I need help.
- God, I shouldn't be feeling this way about somebody of the same sex and I need help.
- God, I know if I make this phone call or send this text message, it's going to go down badly and Lord, I need some help.
- God, my marriage is on the rocks. We sleep in separate rooms and we need help.
- God, the reason I am acting up in school is because I want attention. I need help.
- God, I don't know what to do next in my ministry. Lord, I need help.
- God, my loved one died and I'm struggling to hold it together. I need some HELP!

Whatever it is—physical pain, financial need, your car acting up, feelings of exhaustion—can you be unashamed today to lift your hands and declare, "Lord, I'm struggling and I need some help!" God knows what you need before you ask Him. He's just waiting for you to cry out to Him to do it, fix it, rearrange it, cut it off, make it stop, shrink it!

Jeremiah's complaint shows us there is power available right now when you're honest about what's going on.

3. Jeremiah's Constraint

Jeremiah has shown us his confrontation—that is, people will get mad when you stay faithful to God's message. Jeremiah's complaint shows us that there's power in keeping it real with God and ourselves. This portion of the narrative also shows us Jeremiah's constraint. The definition of "constrain" is to "compel toward a course of action." Picture all of the emotions from Jeremiah's confrontation and complaint pushed into a 2-liter soda bottle. The bottle narrows at the top and those emotions become constrained. In essence, Jeremiah uses what his enemies have caused him to go through as fuel for his future. Verse 9 says that Jeremiah got so down and discouraged that he considered no longer preaching God's message, nor would he even speak about God anymore. Basically, he said, "These folks have talked smack about me for the last time. I've been the butt of the last joke. Nobody will get to blame me for stuff I didn't say and stuff I didn't do. I'm taking my marbles, hanging up my sandals, and I'm going back home." Remember the television series *Cheers*? The theme song declared that "Sometimes you wanna go where everybody knows your name." I imagine that's what Jeremiah was feeling. But then, all of the sudden, something got to moving on the inside of him. He doesn't tell us exactly what he felt, because this feeling was beyond his imagination.

He began to feel something that made him want to run on just a little while longer. He began to feel something that put some pep in his step. God gave him some Gatorade in the fourth quarter and he began to feel like playing the rest of the game! He began to realize that the fire may have gone out, but the flame was still lit. He began to realize that his troubles would not be his demise. He got tired of holding it all back and he finally said, "Oh my God! What's in me is greater than what's against me! I'm tired of holding it back. I'm tired of the enemy in me telling me that I won't make it! I'm tired of the enemy saying that I'm nothing but a joke. I'm tired of the enemy thinking God's word is irrelevant."

I can't help but to keep pursuing excellence in God because when I try to hold it back, it's like FIRE shut up in my bones! Have you ever had a "fire in your bones" experience? You tried to give up, you tried to give in, but God said, "The best is yet to come!" And suddenly it was like fire shut up in your bones.

You tried to give up on your kids, on your marriage, on your church, on your pastor, but God said, "I refuse to let you be average." And then it was like fire shut up in your bones. I'm so glad that God doesn't need matches to start that fire or to keep me going! As long as I have the Lord in my heart, He is fire all by himself!

Come with me back to the truck stop. When I saw that it was late at night, my daddy was tired, we were low on fuel, and he had left the truck running, I did the only logical thing. I woke my daddy up.

"Daddy!" I said. "Wake up! You left the truck running. We're going to run out of gas."

He replied, "Boy, go to sleep. This truck runs on diesel fuel. It burns slower than unleaded gasoline. We've got enough to make it through the night."

Stop tossing and turning, my friend. Lay down and get some sleep. You don't have to worry about running out of fuel because if you've got that One somebody in your life, you don't burn like other people do. *God don't need no matches* to keep your fire lit! That fire will never go out, and I'm glad that what was shut up in the crucifixion sprang into a FIRE of redemption in the resurrection. I thank God for Jesus! I thank God for my Lord! God don't need no matches cause He's fire all by Himself!

Closing prayer:

God, I thank You for the fire you bring. Thank You for the man from Galilee who set me free. He saved my soul and made me whole. Give me fire to testify for You in this sin-ridden world. Thank You Jesus for loving me first. Thank You for being the fire that consumes Satan's plans for my destruction. Give me Jeremiah-like resolve and the fire to never give up. Amen.

9 - Forgiveness at the Cross

"Then said Jesus, Father, forgive them; for they know not what they do. And they parted his raiment, and cast lots."

Luke 23:34

IN 2010, THE Centers for Disease Control and Prevention reported that there were approximately 2.5 million deaths in the United States. Of these 2.5 million deaths, here were the leading reported causes:

Heart disease - 597,689
Cancer - 574,743
Chronic lower respiratory disease - 138,080
Stroke - 129,476
Accidents - 120,859
Alzheimer's disease - 83,494
Diabetes - 69,071
Nephritis, nephrotic syndrome, nephrosis - 50,476
Influenza and pneumonia - 50,097
Suicide - 38,364

As distressing and disquieting as these statistics may be, there is another silent killer whose statistics are not reported by the CDC, but whose symptoms are all too obvious. Brother or sister, believe it or not, countless numbers of people are physically, mentally, emotionally, and spiritually dying slow deaths from the devastating effects of unforgiveness.

What is unforgiveness? I'm glad you asked. Unforgiveness is lacking the ability or desire to change your attitude for the better toward a person, institution, or system that has hurt you. It is a deliberate mindset to resent the wrong and the wrong-doer, and consciously desire revenge. Here are some ways this might manifest itself in a person's life:

- Mean attitudes or actions toward someone because that person reminds you of someone who has hurt you in the past.
- You don't believe a child will amount to anything because of his or her "no good" mama or daddy.
- You refuse to have anything to do with an institution or organization because of how you were treated 10, 25, or even 40 years ago.
- You treat people of an entire race or gender a certain way because of one person's past actions against you.
- You believe the lie from the pit of hell that God wants you to continue to beat yourself up over a past mistake, instead of receiving what Jesus Christ died for and turning away from your sin to a newness of life.

Unforgiveness is the single most popular poison that the enemy uses against God's people because the devil knows that when the unforgiving heart clings to hurts of the past it's difficult, even impossible, to extend the grace to ourselves and others that God has so freely extended to us. I'm so grateful for the good news pronounced by the hymnologist of old for those struggling with this disease of unforgiveness. As Isaac Watts struggled to fully understand the forgiveness offered to him through Jesus Christ, his eyes were fully opened and he said:

Alas! And did my Savior bleed,
And did my Sovereign die?
Would He devote that sacred head,
For such a worm as I?
At the cross, at the cross where I first saw the light,
And the burden of my heart rolled away,
It was there by faith I received my sight,
And now I am happy all the day!

Luke 23:34 is tailored to teach us that it is possible to forgive ourselves and forgive others when we focus on the forgiveness Jesus offers us at the cross.

Live on the scene in this text we find one of the most dramatic, climactic scenes in the entire New Testament. The Jesus who came down through 42 generations to be born of a virgin and her betrothed husband; the Jesus who opened the eyes of the blind, the ears of the deaf, and loosened the tongues of the mute; the Jesus who turned water into wine and grew His disciples' faith by making a fish fry for thousands out of nothing but leftovers... that Jesus is seen here dying on a cross. He was placed between two convicted criminals on a hill called Golgotha—the place of the skull—called such because of the way the hill protruded from the ground like a head from a man's body. Jesus is dying on the cross.

I'd like to pause here parenthetically and note that Jesus' death was both natural and unnatural. It was natural in that is was a real death. The records say that when this real suffering took place, this real man died, His real body was placed in a real tomb, where real women came on the third day to discover His real body was really not there. Jesus death was natural in that it was a real death.

It was unnatural in the sense that it was an abnormal death. The Bible says that the wages of sin is death, however, Jesus was sinless. Death was unnatural for Him. So Jesus' death was both natural and unnatural. The reality of the events of His death is the first of three places we will look as we examine the path to forgiveness.

1. We are called to forgive ourselves and others in the middle of the most unforgivable situations

The first three words of our verse read: *"Then said Jesus..."* They may not seem like much, but they begin to mean a whole lot for your life if you consider what the "then" in the text means. "Then" is a positioning or qualifying word that gives indication as to the order of something happening. When we see a "then" in Scripture, we'd do well to tap into our inner Inspector Gadget and find out what happened earlier that the "then" is referring to. In this case, what happened is that man had done his worst to Jesus. The One by whom the world was made had come into the world, yet the world knew Him not. The Lord of glory had tabernacle among men, but He was not wanted. At His birth, there was no room for Him at the inn and now, there was no room for Him in His persecutors' hearts. A mock trial had been completed, His judges found no fault in Him, yet those who hated Him screamed, "Crucify Him!"

A death with intense suffering had been decided upon. He was whipped with an instrument of leather, glass shards, and nails until flesh was torn and flung from His back. He was nailed to a crossbeam and placed on an upright piece of wood. The entire structure was then lifted up and dropped into a shallow hole in the ground. All the while Jesus hung there, struggling to breathe. It was "THEN," in Jesus' final moments that He prayed to the Father to forgive His foes. Can we agree that if Jesus can ask for those enemies to be forgiven in the middle of that situation, following that brutality and injustice, that somewhere inside of us we possess the capacity to do the same?

It's not easy, but it's possible.

You may have to scream and cry out to God in prayer, but it's possible.

You may have to struggle with whether or not you have the strength to make that phone call, but it's possible.

I don't want you to get it twisted, because sometimes we're not the ones being crucified and struggling to pray for the forgiveness of others. Sometimes we are the ones doing the crucifying. If that's your testimony, I want to encourage you with an eternal exhortation to put down the nails and the hammer before it's everlastingly too late. The Bible says that God is a jealous, protective Father, and He does not take kindly to you crucifying His children. Put the nails and hammer down. Stop the terrorizing. God's forgiveness is offered to you as well, but you've got to receive it. Sometimes we are called to forgive ourselves and others in the middle of the most unforgivable situations.

2. The beginning of authentic Christian forgiveness is prayer

Luke 23:34 begins, *"Then said Jesus, Father..."* In His final moments, Jesus made an intentional decision to have a personal conversation with His Father. If you're going to be biblically sound and authentic on your journey of forgiveness, you've got to resolve that even though you might be angry with yourself, with your child's mother or father, with a system or institution, or with someone to whom you've stopped talking, you won't stop talking to your Heavenly Daddy about it. Jesus' intercession lays the basis for God's offer of post-resurrection forgiveness. Whatever decisions you make on your journey of forgiveness need to flow from your conversation with the Father. If you aren't careful you'll trade what could have been a victory into a great loss due to vindictiveness. The Lord says, "Vengeance is mine." A conversation with the Father will not only remind you of that, but also:

- That you wrestle not against flesh and blood, but against principalities, against powers, against the rulers of the darkness of this world and against spiritual wickedness.
- That weeping may endure for a night, but joy comes in the morning.
- That you can't stoop down to the level of those that persecute you because the fruits of the Spirit are love, joy, peace, patience, kindness, goodness, faithfulness, gentleness, and self-control.
- That you can say, "God bless you" instead of cussing somebody out.
- That you can stay planted where you should be instead of stepping out to where you shouldn't.
- That you can say what David did in Psalm 35: "Even though ruthless witnesses come forward: they question me on things I know nothing about. They repay me evil for good and leave me like one bereaved. STILL, I will give you thanks in the great assembly; among the throngs I will praise you."

Those are good words if you find yourself looking in the mirror, knowing that you are being pushed close to the edge. If you are angry and hurt, don't cut 'em, don't cuss 'em. You just keep talking to the Father about bad people and bad problems. I guarantee that God will do something about it.

In Acts 16:25-26, we read about some godly people dealing with some earthly issues. The Bible says, "And at midnight Paul and Silas prayed, and sang praises unto God: and the prisoners heard them. And suddenly there was a great earthquake, so that the foundations of the prison were shaken: and immediately all the doors were opened and every one's bands were loosed."

Did Paul and Silas cuss the guards? Did they disrespect the guards? Did they give them a piece of their minds? No. They PRAYED and SANG PRAISES unto God. And if you want to loosen the bands of unforgiveness, I dare you to have a little talk with Jesus about it. Tell Him. Sing praises to Him. Pray intently, even in the middle of the problem. The beginning and the end of authentic Christian forgiveness is prayer!

3. Supernatural strength flows when you forgive those who hurt you

Let's look next at what Jesus said in Luke 23:34, *"Then said Jesus, Father, forgive them; for they know not what they do."*

Who was Jesus speaking about? He asked God to forgive both those who actively supported His death and those passively supporting His death. Jesus did not say what criminals were supposed to say as they were put to death, "May my death atone for all my sins." No, remember this was an unnatural death, Jesus was sinless and was dying for the sins of others, so He confesses the sins of those who falsely crucified Him. This was an affirmation of what He had prayed in the Garden of Gethsemane, "Father let this cup pass from me, but not my will but thine be done."

Jesus' plea for the forgiveness of His persecutors gave Him the strength to stay on the cross and do what He knew He had to do for you and for me. The record says that HE was wounded for our transgressions and bruised for our iniquity, and though the chastisement of our peace was upon Him, with His stripes we are not educated, motivated, or inspired, but we are healed.

He was punished that we might be forgiven.
He was wounded that we might be healed.
He was made sin to declare us righteous.
He died that we might receive life.
He endured poverty for our abundance.
He bore our shame for His glory.
He was rejected for our acceptance.
He was cursed that we might be blessed.

I am so thankful the record doesn't stop there, cause the same man who was falsely accused, whipped, beaten, and who died did not stay dead. Three days later the report came that He was not in the tomb, but He had risen from the dead.

There is forgiveness for your sins. There is power you can draw from to forgive others. It is found at the cross.

Closing prayer:

Lord Jesus, I confess to You that forgiving is hard. I want to hold on to the hurts and sins of others. I want to be the one to see revenge on my enemies. I want to be angry at those who have wronged me or my family. I repent of my anger. I repent of my unforgiveness. I ask You to wash me clean from my own sins of unforgiveness and I pray to walk forward with a forgiving heart that seeks to be like Yours. Amen.

10 - Giving God Your Best

"Therefore I thought it necessary to exhort the brethren, that they would go before unto you, and make up beforehand your bounty, whereof ye had notice before, that the same might be ready, as a matter of bounty, and not as of covetousness. But this I say, He which soweth sparingly shall reap also sparingly; and he which soweth bountifully shall reap also bountifully. Every man according to as he purposeth in his heart, so let him give; not grudingly, or of necessity: for God loveth a cheerful giver. And God is able to make all grace abound toward you; that ye, always having all sufficiency in all things, may abound to every good work:"

2 Corinthians 9:5-8

IT WAS THE second half of a long soccer match. The game was tied and the crowd was on its feet. My body was exhausted and my breathing grew shallow. I remember bending over, with my hands on my knees. I looked over to my coach and mouthed the words, "Can you take me out of the game? I'm tired."

As exhausted as I was, do you know what she said to me? She said, "Kan'Dace, there are two minutes left. I know you're tired, but you have to keep going."

In that moment, in a crucial part of the game, I acknowledged that I had to give my best. My teammates, fully aware of my condition and my need for a breather, continued to rally around me. In the last minute of that match, my teammate passed me the ball and I kicked it into the goal for the winning score. My body was wracked with fatigue, but I was determined to give my best to the end.

Might I dare to ask you: In this game called life, are you giving God your best? Even when your month is longer than your money? Even when your change is strange? Even when you are ready to be taken out of the game? It is in those last two minutes you must think of the goodness of Jesus and all He has done, and you'll find that you can't help but want to give Him your best. Yes, in all you do, whether with your time, talents, or your treasures, you should give your all to God. You can give your best to God because God has given His best to you.

Now before you check out on me, thinking you can't possibly bear to read another message about giving, I want to assure you that God has a word for you in this teaching.

Many scholars believe that Second Corinthians was written by the Apostle Paul with the assistance of Timothy. It was during that time, roughly 55 AD, that Paul wrote several letters to the early churches. We see in the first 7 chapters of this epistle that Paul is dealing with housekeeping issues with the Corinthians. In chapter 8, Paul applauds the efforts of the Macedonian churches. The Macedonians were under great stress, but when asked to give to the church in Jerusalem, they gave above and beyond Paul's expectation. Paul knew the finances were needed to address the famine, war, and poverty that plagued Jerusalem. Though the Macedonians were going through their own struggles, Paul was able to write about them (in verse 5), "And they exceeded our expectations: They gave themselves first of all to the Lord, and then by the will of God also to us."

You see, the churches in Macedonia were committed to giving God their best because they knew God would take care of the rest. Paul told of the generosity of the church at Corinth. Their ability and desire to give to the believers in Jerusalem not only met the needs of fellow believers, but also excited the churches at Macedonia to continue in their giving. Your giving, or lack thereof, could be affecting someone else's desire to give, and you may not even know it.

As chapter 8 wraps up, we learn that Paul sent Titus and the brethren to remind the Corinthians of the tangible, generous gift they are to send to Jerusalem. The church of Corinth could have been offended by Titus and the brethren's reminder. We see in chapter 9 that they already had a readiness to give, and yet Paul made sure they were reminded of it. Giving is a spiritual discipline, and we all need to be reminded to be ready to give.

1. You have to plan to give

In verse 5, we read that Paul urges the Corinthians to plan. He tells them that he thought it was necessary to urge the brothers to visit in advance and finish the arrangements for the generous gift they had promised. Then the giving would be readily, and not grudgingly, given at the last minute.

Paul reminded them to plan because he knew that life could get the better of them, thus shifting their focus from giving generously to giving begrudgingly. It is in this principle that life gets real for us sometimes, too. We know that even in our moments of giving, life happens. For example, you might purpose in your heart to give a little more to your church, but then your gas bill is higher than expected. Or you want to donate to a charity around Christmastime, but your car needs new tires.

Child of God, I know times get tough, but even when life happens, you have to listen to what Paul tells the church at Corinth and stay committed to your plan to give God your best. Why? Because your plan to give is connected to God giving His best back to you.

2. You have to understand the principles of giving

A principle is defined as a fundamental law or truth on which others are based. Another way to think of a principle is to think of a rule, a law, or a method. For example, one commonly known physics law (Newton's Third Law) states that for every action there is an equal and opposite reaction. A general principle of gravity states that what goes up, must come down. We know these basic things. But, are you familiar with God's principles for giving?

Have a look at verse 6 of our text. Simply stated, it means, "When you give a little, you get a little. When you give a lot, you get a lot."

Take a moment to look at your life. You keep wondering if God hears your prayer, but how much time are you giving to God in prayer? You don't understand why your days are full of trouble or frustration, but I ask, did you wake up with God on your mind or was He an afterthought?

Galatians 6 is another place where we are told that we reap what we sow. Ask yourself: Am I sowing? What am I sowing? Good ground gives good harvest.

3. You have to acknowledge that giving takes preparation

I like how verse 7 reads in the NIV: "Each of you should give what you have decided in your heart to give, not reluctantly or under compulsion, for God loves a cheerful giver."

Paul says that giving has to be decided upon in your heart. He didn't say to decide according to your finances. He did not say to consult your fellow members on how much the Joneses are giving. Paul says that giving begins in the heart.

Speaking of the heart, a few months ago I heard a sermon that dealt with matters of the heart. The speaker shared the story of her son's fatal heart condition, and how necessary it was for her other children to be checked for this same ailment because the problem stemmed from a genetic abnormality. When the problem was discovered in her son, she could then be proactive and have her other children checked. Sadly, the reality for us is that our lack of preparation for giving is a heart problem. You have to be aware of the condition of your heart in order to make an informed decision in your giving.

Do you desire the church to meet your every need, but hold back yourself when it comes to giving to the needs of others? Do you hold on to anger or jealousy against your fellow brothers and sisters? Yes, others will make you mad from time to time, but allow God to conduct a heart transplant on you so you can give as God desires you to do.

At the end of verse 7 we read that God loves a cheerful giver. He doesn't say He loves a giver with pockets as deep as Lake Michigan or as wide as Texas. He doesn't love a giver that can pay for the entire church to go to dinner. He loves a cheerful giver.

The word cheerful in the Greek language translates to *hilaros*, which means merry, hilarious, prompt, willing. If we insert those definitions back into the text we see that God desires a prompt and willing giver who does so with merriment in his or her heart. This includes giving of your resources and also of yourself. Giving God your best takes preparation.

4. There is purpose in your giving

Verse 8 reads, "And God is able to make all grace abound toward you; that ye, always having all sufficiency in all things, may abound to every good work:"

The promise I gain from this verse and I want you to see also is that when you purposely give to God, your needs will be taken care of. Not some of your needs, but in all things, having all that you need. When you give God your time, your talent, and your treasure, you can trust that He's got everything worked out.

We don't serve an accidental God. He is purposeful. When you give as He prompts and instructs us to do, He will allow whatever you gave to Him to cover and be greater than you can even imagine, in both your natural and spiritual lives.

Romans 8:28 shows that in all things God works for the good of those who love Him, who have been called according to His purpose. This means, in all that you do or go through or encounter, you can know that it will all work out for your good.

Hear me, beloved: God can work out all things for a good purpose.

I am reminded of a story of a young woman whose father recently died. In the days leading up to his death, he called each of his children to him, had them lean over his bedside, and he would whisper seemingly random words such as, "desk, mattress, closet."

The children did not pay much mind to these odd utterances. After he passed, while they gathered and reminisced their memories, the subject of the random words came up. The mother reminded the children of the father's squirrelish tendencies, and how he would hide things in strange places. They looked into the places he'd mentioned and found that what appeared to be nonsense words by a dying man were actually commands to find large sums of money and instructions. In their sorrow, the family discovered that even though their father died, he had left them his best.

That earthly father left his best behind for his children, and I am reminded of another who gave us His best. That man was Jesus. Jesus came to earth, born of a virgin girl over two thousand years ago because God wanted to give us His best.

He laid in a borrowed tomb for three days because He wanted to give us His best.

Bright and early that third day morning, God raised Him from the dead because He wanted to give us His best.

And because God gave us His best, I dare you to give God yours. I dare you to say, "Father, I am planning my praise for you because I want to give you my best."

Tell Him now that you understand the principles, you know it takes preparation, and you know there is a purpose in your giving, because you can't out-give Him, no matter how hard you try.

Back on that soccer field, I almost threw in the towel. But I stayed in the game and got to taste the sweet victory. What victories are awaiting you, if you would only determine to always give God your best?

Closing prayer:

Father, I commit my very best to You today. Remind me often to be purposeful in giving to You my time, my talent, and my treasure. Thank You for showing me the model I am to follow in my giving. I place all that I have into Your loving hands. Amen.

11 - Dealing with Divine Delays

"Then Martha said unto Jesus, Lord, if thou hadst been here, my brother had not died. But I know, that even now, whatsoever thou wilt ask of God, God will give it thee. Jesus saith unto her, Thy brother shall rise again."

John 11:21-23

ONE SUNDAY, I sprinted out of the pulpit to catch a flight from Grand Rapids, Michigan to San Antonio, Texas. I had orders to report to Lackland Air Force Base the very next day and as much as it was up to me, I was determined that I wasn't going to miss my flight. However, no sooner than I made my concluding remarks and pronounced the benediction, I began to experience what I like to call progressive periods of postponement... also known as delays.

Beloved, before I could make it to the church parking lot, I got stopped by a good 'ol church mother, one of my most senior members, that had a question that just couldn't wait till the following week, but y'all, I wasn't worried... because to me, this interruption was just a minor delay. I managed to make it to the airport, only to find that I was the last car in a long line of about 20 cars trying to make it to the entrance for departing passengers. But I still wasn't worried 'cause this was just a minor delay. And after inchin' my car forward, and makin' it to the airport entrance, huggin' my wife goodbye and sprinting into the airport... I made it to the check-in line only to find the line wrapped around the corner. As I looked at my watch, wiping the sweat off my forehead... I still wasn't worried because my presence in this long line only represented a minor delay.

I got my ticket, and made it to security only to find that the same people from the check-in line had mysteriously followed me to the security line. As a matter of fact, they beat me there. As I looked at the zig-zagging line that seemed to go on and on and on, I *still* wasn't worried because the zig-zagging line without an end was still just a minor delay.

What messed me up was what happened when I finally made it to my departure gate. After rushing out the pulpit, miraculously making it past a church mother, inchin' my car slowly to the airport entrance while switching my foot a thousand times from the brake pedal to the gas pedal and back to the brake pedal again, wiping the sweat off my forehead, waiting patiently in the check-in line, and making it through airport security, a voice came over the loud speaker system that said, "We apologize for the inconvenience, but due to unforeseen circumstances, the plane has not arrived and this flight has been delayed."

I stood there in disbelief. I didn't know what was going on with the airline—nor did I care—all I knew was that the plane that I needed to be on had not showed up. And if I might say, in this existential situation called life, there will be times when you find yourself perplexed as a result of having experienced progressive periods of postponement... also known as delays. You've been there before. You worked hard to be at the right place at the right time, you had the ticket in your hand confirming that you'd paid your dues and you deserved to be sitting in a designated seat on your way to your destiny. You even made it miraculously through things that took other folks out, but still circumstances beyond your control came over the loud speaker system of life only to let you know that what you so desperately needed to lift you off seemed to have let you down by simply not showing up. And times like these cause us to consider an interesting interrogative that can be translated into the relevant question... "How do you handle life when it seems like our omnipresent God, One who is able to be everywhere at all times, is not where you need Him to be?" Or better yet, what do you do, how do you cope, when you see everybody else...

Being blessed
Getting married
Starting new jobs
Being delivered
With well-behaved children
Getting along with their spouses
Able to pay their bills

Recognized for their hard work

However, when it comes to your deliverance, it seems like God forgot your address. Here you are, hair falling out, blood pressure going up, can't sleep at night, jacked up diet, about to lose your everlasting mind because you're dealing with progressive periods of postponement—divine delays.

This message is here to encourage you that if you hang in there, beloved, God will get the glory out of your story. Because one thing I know is that God always has a redemptive purpose in His divine delay. The Divine will often use a delay of His manifestation to make a great impact through a future demonstration.

"Preacher, what are you saying?" you might wonder.

I'm saying God's timing is always the right timing. The silver saints said it this way, "He may not come when you want Him, but He's always on time. He's an on-time God; yes, He is!"

And I want to encourage you today that whatever it is you're waiting on God to work out, keep hanging in there because God has not lost your address. The Lord knows where you live. Keep turning the pages of time because your story is yet being written. If you don't remember anything else from this message, remember that God always gets the glory out of a Divine delay.

The text I want to examine is found in the 11th chapter of the gospel according to John. You know who John is, don't you? John is the one who kicks off his gospel with the epic declaration, "In the beginning was the Word, and the Word was with God, and the Word was God. The same was in the beginning with God. All things were made by him; and without him was not any thing made that was made. In him was life; and the life was the light of men."

This same man records in chapter eleven that Jesus has received word from Bethany that Lazarus, the son of Simon and the brother of His friends Martha and Mary, is not just ill, but he is sick unto death. And strangely, so it seems, as much as Jesus loved Lazarus, as deep as the connection was between the three siblings and Jesus, after hearing of the severity of Lazarus' illness, Jesus delays His journey to Bethany by two days. When Jesus finally arrives in Bethany, He is confronted by Martha. It is in the conversation that follows this confrontation that we find strength to cope with and deal with Divine delays. I want to examine three aspects of Martha's experience.

1. Martha was bothered by Jesus' absence (v.21)
2. Martha had faith in Jesus' ability (v. 22)
3. Martha was given Jesus' assurance (v. 23)

1. Jesus' Absence

In verse 21 we see that Martha was bothered by the absence of Jesus. She basically says, "Jesus, I've been texting you for four days, and you haven't texted me back! Jesus, didn't you get my e-mails? Didn't you get my phone calls? Lord, didn't you see me trolling your Twitter feed? Didn't Facebook update you on Lazarus' status? Did you not see the Instagram pics from the funeral? Lord, if you had been here, Lazarus would not have died!"

And in Martha's frustration we discover that if we are going to deal with Divine delays, we've got to be honest with ourselves and admit that there are times when we are bothered by what feels like God's absence. We've got to look into our spirits and admit that dire circumstances often cause us to doubt God's timing. We feel like saying, "God, if you had been here...

I'd still have my job."
my mama wouldn't have died."
I wouldn't be divorced."
circumstances would be different."
I wouldn't feel locked up, tied up, and fed up."

God sent me to you with a public service announcement to let you know that His patient purpose will not stumble during our attempts to guilt-trip Him as we grieve. God does not always operate on clocks and calendars like we do. God operates on revelation and truth. In fact, Isaiah notes in chapter 55, verse 8 that God's thoughts are nothing like our thoughts and His ways are far beyond anything we could imagine. When God, in His sovereignty, in His "God-ness," determines that it is the right time to move and when He determines that it's the appropriate season to manifest His power, then He will step onto the stage of your life and show up and show out. Until then, guess what? You've got to wait and realize that the first step in the healing process, the first step in dealing with a Divine delay is being real with yourself and admitting that there are times when you are bothered by what you perceive to be God's absence.

A few days ago I was talking with a friend of mine that had done an intervention of sorts with a family. The mother and father were at their wits' end with their seventeen year old daughter. After about an hour and a half into this intervention that seemed to be going nowhere, my friend said to the daughter, "Can I cut to the chase and ask you an honest question? Do you feel loved by your parents?"

The stoic seventeen year old young lady, who had hardly said a word in an hour and a half, broke down into tears as she began to detail how she had not felt loved by her parents in ten years, since the birth of her younger brother. She felt like he'd stolen all of her parents' attention and she had been rebelling against them to get some of that attention back. And amazingly, it was only moments later that the family hugged and agreed to take further steps to continue meeting with a counselor to heal as a family. I want you to see that this only took place when the one at the center of the frustration made the honest admission that she was bothered by what she perceived to be the emotional absence of her parents. And that's a word for you, if you bear the miserable weight of frustration on your shoulders. You've got to realize that the first step in solving a problem is admitting that you have one. And I believe that if we really knew that God is big enough to handle our frustration, we'd get to a quiet place sometime and really tap into our personal relationship with Him and say, "God, it really bothered me when:

I prayed and the door that I thought would open stayed closed."

I got down on my knees and it seemed my situation got worse."

I dialed your number and it seemed like you didn't pick up."

Here's the good news. I heard my good friend Pastor Hodari Hamilton say when we're honest with God in prayer, we're not so much informing Him (because He already knows), as we are inviting Him to have His way in our circumstances. In essence, when we (as God's creation) begin to be honest with our Creator, we admit that, "God, nobody can fix this but you." Life is not so much about having all the answers as it is learning to live with the questions.

One thing I know is that God will give you grace to live life's unanswered questions. There's healing power in the honest admission to the Almighty that sometimes you are bothered by what you perceive to be His absence.

2. Jesus' Ability

What I love about this passage is that while the text says that Martha was bothered by Jesus' absence, the Apostle John also shows us that Martha maintained faith in Jesus' ability. Beloved, let me encourage you that when you're dealing with a Divine delay you might stop doing some of the things you would normally do, but don't you ever lose faith in God's ability. Even if you've got to get some professional help to cope with a really hard situation, don't lose faith in God's ability! Don't lose knowledge of the abiding reality that God has the power to work it out! I'm not lying to you. Watch the text in verse 22. Martha says, "But I know, that even now, whatsoever thou wilt ask of God, God will give it thee."

Martha recognized that even though her brother had been dead as a doornail for four days, Jesus still had a hook up for her hang up. Martha believed that because she was connected to Jesus, and Jesus is connected to God, even as the stench of her brother's death was permeating the grave, Jesus could still turn this mess into a miracle. And that's why I love the natural progression of this text, because we see in the narrative flow that Martha's affirmation in Jesus' ability testified that even as she grieved she didn't become so fixated on her frustration that she allowed it to hinder her faith. The text says that after all Martha and her family had been through in the last four days, something in her gave her the strength to keep her faith moving forward.

This kind of reminds me of the first car that I had. It was a 1984 Oldsmobile Cutlass. Y'all, it was clean! It had a fresh pearly white paint job, tinted windows, boomin' sound system, and rims that cost more than the car. I thought I was, as they say, "all that and a bag of chips." However, one day I got in my car, popped it in gear, and the transmission started acting up. The only gear that it would go in was reverse. So, if you know me, you'll not be surprised that since I only had about one block to drive to a friend's house, I drove it in reverse for the whole block. However, before I got out of my car, my car started preaching to me.

My car said, "Fred."

I said, "Yeah, car. What's up?"

My car said, "Turn the music down so you can hear me."

I said, "My bad. Talk to me."

My car said, "Fred, I want you to know something. We made it down the block, but I wasn't built to drive backwards."

I said, "OK Mr. Car, that sounds good, but what do you mean?"

My car said, "I have a rearview mirror so I can be reminded of what's around me, but my windshield is bigger than my rearview mirror because I'm built to take you forward."

And in that illustration, my old '84 Cutlass blessed me that day. You see, we can't get so stuck living in the reverse circumstances of life that we forget that we are built to live forward. There might be some stuff that needs to be fixed, and it might even take us in reverse for a little while. But oh, when we fix our minds on Jesus' ability, we can begin to move forward. When you're dealing with a Divine delay, dealing with a dead situation, you've got to be like Martha and have an "even now" theology that says:

- I know I'm struggling right now, and it looks like I'm not going to make it, but even now Jesus can fix it.
- The bills need to be paid and the kids have needs to be met, but even now Jesus can fix it.
- My anxiety is so bad that I can't hold down a meal, but even now Jesus can fix it.
- When it gets thick, all my friends thin out, but even now Jesus can fix it.

You might stop doing a whole lot of things, but don't you ever lose faith in Jesus' ability.

3. Jesus' Assurance

Martha has shown us that when we're dealing with Divine delays, there will be times when we're bothered by what we perceive to be God's absence, but even in the midst of this, we must maintain faith in God's ability. However, the text further encourages us that when we're experiencing a progressive period of postponement, we can have confidence in Jesus' blessed assurance. In verse 23, the Bible says that Jesus tells Martha, "Thy brother shall rise again." Now, as twenty-first century believers, that's good news for us because we know this whole narrative. However, Martha's response in verse 24 indicates she believed Jesus to be affirming the traditional Jewish hope of the resurrection of the dead at the end of the current age, not the assurance that Jesus could and would raise her brother right now.

In 1 Thessalonians 4:16-17, Paul speaks of this resurrection when he says, "For the Lord Himself will descend from heaven with a shout, with the voice of the archangel and with the trumpet of God, and the dead in Christ will rise first. Then we who are alive and remain will be caught up together with them in the clouds to meet the Lord in the air, and so we shall always be with the Lord."

And friends, I'm grateful that because of my confession of faith in the death, burial, and resurrection of Jesus Christ, I'll be there on that great resurrection day. But, I'm also grateful that this text is tailored to teach us that in the meantime, when we are forced to deal with situations beyond our control, Jesus has the power not only to resurrect us in the future, but He can also resuscitate and bring some stuff back to life right now. And sometimes, you just need to go to your prayer closet and say, "Lord, I'm grateful that You have the power to fulfill some things in the future, but I also celebrate the assurance that I have in You that, if You choose to, You can speak the word and some stuff that's been dead and cried over can be brought back to life."

God will give you strength to deal with Divine delays!

Closing Prayer:

Father, I've had times when I am frustrated because I doubt whether You hear me or see my problems. Let me go forward encouraged and strengthened in the ability and assurance of Your power. Remind me that You are never absent. Thank You, God that Your time is always on time. Amen.

12 - A Theology of Suffering

"And lest I should be exalted above measure through the abundance of the revelations, there was given to me a thorn in the flesh, the messenger of Satan to buffet me, lest I should be exalted above measure. For this thing I besought the Lord thrice, that it might depart from me. And he said unto me, My grace is sufficient for thee: for my strength is made perfect in weakness. Most gladly therefore I will rather glory in my infirmities, that the power of Christ may rest upon me."

2 Corinthians 12:7-9

"THEOS" MEANS GOD. "Ology" means the study of something. You put these 2 words together and you have what would seem to be "the study of God." However, no one can really study the unsurpassable, insurmountable being that is God. In fact, theologian Anselm of Canterbury describes God as "a being than which none greater can be conceived." A simple working definition of theology suggests that theology is (GET THIS) an orderly way of thinking about God. I would dare say that even if you never quite figure out why or how God does what He does, there is power in putting yourself in a position to think about it. Because if you don't at least think about how God works, you'll turn around one day and find out that you have been making life-altering decisions based on what you *heard* instead of what you *know* for yourself; specifically as it pertains to how you act and react in times of suffering. Consider these lyrics:

- "I sing because I'm happy, I sing because I'm free, His eye is on the sparrow and I know He watches me."
- "Precious Lord, take my hand, lead me on, let me stand, I am tired, I am weak, I am worn, through the storm, through the night, lead me on to the light."
- "The blood that Jesus shed for me way back on Calvary, the

blood that gives me strength from day-to-day, it will never lose its power."

The only reason we can sing the lyrics to these songs is because somebody took the time out to think about how God would have them act and react during the most challenging moments of their lives. And you do know, don't ya', that we are living in some challenging times? We are living in a time when:

- The nuclear family seems to be a thing of the past.
- People are having to make decisions between getting necessities for their household or getting necessities for their healthcare.
- Elementary-aged children are questioning their sexuality.
- People want the benefits of a religion without the responsibility of a relationship with God.

Yes, we are living in some challenging times.

However, the real question is how will you act and react during the most challenging moments of your life? Better yet, is your theology, your orderly way of thinking about God, stable, strong, and sufficient enough to sustain you through times of mental, physical, emotional, and spiritual weakness?

And before we go a step further in this discussion, I want to encourage you that the Spirit of the Lord spoke in my spirit to tell you that God is able use the most challenging moments of your life to shape what you know about Him. And if you don't remember anything else in this chapter, remember that God wants you to have a THEOLOGY of SUFFERING.

In our text, God has something to say about our encounters with suffering. We find the apostle Paul traveling through Macedonia on his way to Corinth in southern Greece. Paul established the church at Corinth during his 18 month stay there in 52 AD, and three years after this establishment, Paul learned that some of the recently converted Christians were having difficulty breaking the habits of their former lifestyle. It was at this moment Paul paused in Ephesus to put his pen to the parchment and write his first letter to the Corinthian church, with detailed instructions on how to live godly lives. However, as Paul continues his trek to Corinth, he saw one of the associate ministers of the Corinthian church, Rev. Titus, traveling northbound. As Titus jumped off his camel, he embraced Paul and greeted him saying, "How are you doing, Pastor Paul? Grace be to you and peace from God our father, and from the Lord Jesus Christ. Let me inform you that your first letter to the Corinthian church was received well and you'd be surprised at the positive changes taking place. The choir just bought new robes and the youth department just completed a successful camel wash to raise money for the Youth Convention trip to Jerusalem. However Pastor, I also have some very troubling news. There is a faction in the church that are questioning whether you are really a called man of God. They are telling the new believers they must convert to Judaism to really be Christians. Now Pastor, I thought that we settled this at the Council of Jerusalem in Acts chapter 15, when we all agreed that God cleanses the heart by faith. However, this faction is emphasizing religion over and above relationship.

"Pastor, something MUST be done quickly because these 'Judaizers,' as they are called, are teaching a theology or an experience with God based on lifting themselves above God's purpose for their lives. Now Pastor, I know I'm talking a lot, but I remember you telling us about how you had been shipwrecked, beaten, stoned, and took 39 stripes, not for yourself, but ALL for the glory of God! Pastor, you taught a theology, an experience with God, focused not on self but focused on going through whatever you have to go through so God can get the glory. Yes Pastor, you taught us a theology of suffering."

Upon hearing this, I imagine Paul paused for a moment near the city of Philippi and decided to write another letter to this Corinthian church that he loved so dearly. However, this letter would be less doctrinal than any other letter that he had written. You see, Paul had a history of disputes with the Jews dating back to Acts chapter 18, so he decided to take a different approach this time; he would try to explain himself more crystal clearly than he had ever done before. Paul decided to pit himself against what these church leaders and church members believed God's intent in our suffering to be.

1. Purpose from your pain

In The Message version of verse 7, Paul says, "Because of the extravagance of those revelations, and so I wouldn't get a big head, I was given the gift of a (thorn in the flesh) a disability to keep me in constant touch with my human limitations." In this, we gather that if you are to embrace a theology of suffering, you must first understand that God is ABLE TO DRAW PURPOSE from YOUR PAIN.

God is able to take what you think is meant to break you and use it to make you. He alone can take what you think is a set-back and use it as a set-up. Friend, God is able to use what would normally take people out and use it to bring you in.

In other words, suffering is a human issue that's able to be used for heaven's intent. That isn't to say God causes our suffering, but in His sovereignty, in His God-ness, He uses our moments of suffering to remind us of our humanity. Verse 7 notes that Paul had something affecting him, be it physical, mental, emotional, or spiritual, that sought to severely hinder the major activity of his life—that being spreading the good news of our risen Savior. At this point, I must pause and say that a great theological debate continues as to what this thorn in the flesh or messenger from Satan actually was. People way smarter than me have asked, "Was it physical or was Paul speaking figuratively?" The scriptural evidence convinces me that Paul's thorn was most likely these antagonizing Judaizers because the Greek word in verse 8 meaning "to take away" is used throughout the New Testament referring to persons and not things.

And can I just say, it is one thing to be sick in your body, but quite another to be sick of those "thorn in your flesh" kind of people. There are some people that'll do stuff that just gets on your last nerve. But, regardless of what this thorn in the flesh or messenger of Satan was, according to the Bible, it was deemed necessary to keep Paul grounded. Notice also that the words "torment me" in verse seven are in the grammatical present tense which implies frequents attacks or an acute recurrent obstacle. Paul told the Corinthian church that God gave him something so painful and such a hindrance to spreading the good news of Jesus Christ that it would seem to be the work of the devil. Nevertheless, it would Greek *koliphizo* or buffet him, which literally means to "punch with the fist," at various times to keep Paul from becoming spiritually arrogant.

Christian apologist Jerome compared God's use of our suffering to the use of the slave behind the victorious Roman commander. In ancient Rome, a phrase is said to have been used on the occasions when a Roman general was being paraded through the streets of

Rome during a victory celebration known as a triumph. Standing behind the victorious general was a slave, and he had the task of reminding the general that, though he was up on the peak today, tomorrow was another day in which he could fall. The servant did this by telling the general that he should remember that he was but a man. The slave would say, "Memento mori." And, if I could transport these words from the streets of Rome and down the streets of your life, I would advise you to *memento mori*; remember that you are but a man. Remember that:

- Because you are a Christian, people will seek you for spiritual counsel, but remember that you are but a man.
- Because of your position in your household and in your community, people will elevate you, but remember that you are but a man.
- Because of your beauty, brains and personality, because you are handsome, because you are fine, because you are all that and a bag a' chips... the opposite sex will flock to you, but BEFORE YOU TAKE IT "THAT" far (however THAT FAR is), remember that you are but a man.

And at this point, sadly, I must report that good Christian soldiers around the world are falling by the hundreds and by the thousands because, for a few brief moments, they've put down the shield of righteousness, elevated the staff of self-glorification and exposed their hearts to the deadly egotistical arrows of the enemy. My Father's children, God occasions the mountaintop not so you can say, "Look how far I made it," but God occasions the mountaintop so you can have a better view of the valley and be able to say, "Look where He brought me from. He brought me a mighty, mighty long way."

Suffering is a human issue with heavenly intent and God is able to draw purpose from your pain!

2. Power perfected in your weakness

As the candlewick flickered, I imagine Paul launched himself further into this intimate conversation and said, "Corinthian church, not only is God able to draw purpose from your pain, but I want you to know also that God's power is perfected in your weakness."

That is to say that God's miracle workin' power, His *dunamis* is made manifest, it exhibits itself fullest, during the most challenging, weakest moments of our lives.

Let me put it this way, if you are weak, if you are tired of being tired, frustrated with always being frustrated, sick of always bein' sick—then get ready for God's miracle-working power to manifest itself smack in the middle of your situation.

Y'all don't believe me? Listen to my version of Paul in verses 8 and 9, "For this thing I besought the Lord three times—y'all, 3 TIMES—that it (this "thorn in the flesh") would depart from me but God didn't say what I expected Him to say. God didn't say to me, 'Just have faith the size of a mustard seed and go on and toss your thorn into the sea.' No, He said unto me, 'It might get worse before it gets better, but my grace is a grace that will keep you, for my strength is made perfect in weakness.'"

Paul is preparing the Corinthians for a demonstration of the insufficiency of the Judaizers' traditional belief concerning weakness. You see, the number 3 had a special significance in the Jewish community. In fact, three-fold prayers were well-known in Greco-Roman religion and held a special significance to the Gentile believers as well. The scriptures tell us that as Paul prayed, he prayed with the number 3 on his mind. As Paul prayed he probably thought about:

- The three Jewish Patriarchs: Abraham, Isaac, and Jacob. (But this thought could not meet his need.)
- The three leaders of the Jewish nation during their 40 years of wandering in the desert: Moses, Aaron, and Miriam. (But this thought could not meet his need.)
- The significance of the 3 Jewish pilgrim festivals. (But this thought could not meet his need.)
- And, he even thought about the 3 daily Jewish prayer services. (But these 3 designated prayer services could not and would not relieve his pain.)

AND, just as Paul was about to give in, God's voice burst through the agony of his pious petition and said, "Laws and tradition may wither and fade away, but MY grace will sustain you because my power is perfected in your weakness."

And I believe somebody reading this has pressed their hands together, down on their knees in prayer, all day and all night, asking for the thorn to be taken away. You prayed like your Sunday school teacher taught you to pray. You named it and claimed it, but soon learned God could not be manipulated. You went to all the prayer services, you clenched the prayer cloth, but when you got up off your knees, the pain intensified, those hurtful words cut deeper, and depression almost got the best of you.

If this is you, hear me, God's voice bursts through your tearful petition and says, "Keep holding on because my grace will keep you!" And you know what grace is, don't you?

Grace is God's keepin' power. Grace is what puts your weakness in God's focus. Grace puts food on your table. Grace puts money in your pocket. Grace provides a way out of no way. Grace is the miracle wrapped in your skin. Grace is what woke you up this mornin'. Grace is what started you on your way. Grace is that hug you needed. Grace is that text message that lifted you up. Grace is the fact that He's a God of another chance, when your 2nd, 3rd, 4th, and 5th chance ran out. God said, "My grace will keep you because my power is perfected when you are rendered powerless!"

The hymnologist said it this way:

Amazing Grace! How sweet the sound,
That saved a wretch like me!
I once was lost, but now am found;
Was blind, but now I see.

T'was Grace that taught my heart to fear,
And Grace, my fears relieved;
How precious did that Grace appear,
The hour I first believed.

Through many dangers, toils, and snares,
I have already come;
'Tis Grace hath brought me safe thus far,
And Grace will lead me home.

Where would you be if not for His amazing grace?

3. Trade potential for real power

Paul notes that not only does a theology of suffering declare that

God is able to draw purpose from your pain, and that God's power is perfected in your weakness, but as I take this thang' to the bridge, I want you to know that the B portion of verse 9 insists that a solid orderly way of thinking about God during the challenges of life declares that the Lord wants you to trade great potential for real power.

Paul says, "I've got to rejoice about God's grace, I've got to celebrate it so it will rest or dwell in me." Rev. Dr. Charles E. Booth says that we experience God in 3 ways:

1. Vicariously—through others' testimonies.
2. Academically—through study, reflection, and meditation.
3. Practically—in real life, "in living color," if you will.

We learn from Paul that God does not become real unless and until He becomes practical! In this we draw that if the sufficiency of God is going to be fully realized, we've got to engage it, celebrate it, and activate it on a "real life" level. We've got to take the potential and trade it in for power. You see, you've got grace, you've got what you need to make it—JESUS already died and rose again for it—you just need to activate it. You see:

- When you have a light switch in the off position, it's just potential light, but when you flip it up, then you have power.
- When you have a car, it's just a hunk of metal, but when you turn the ignition, then you have power.

You see, your mouth is just your mouth, but when you lift it up in praise, then you have power! Your hands are just your hands, but when you put em' together in prayer, then you have power! Your heart is just your heart, but when you give it to the Lord, then you got power!

Can Jesus get a witness to His complete and all-encompassing power?

Your kids, your spouse, your job, your home, your health, stayin' awake at night, your sin-sick situation is just your situation, but when you TURN IT OVER TO THE LORD... then you've got power! Your mind is just your mind, but when you start thinkin' about Jesus and all that He's done for you, then you have power!

And friend, when you've got Jesus, you've got all the power you need.

Closing Prayer:

Jesus. You give me all the power I need. I confess the times I've let my eyes linger on my situation instead of remembering the power of the heavens that lives inside of me. Forgive me for doubting. Forgive me for trying to do things in my own power. Thank You, Jesus, for the grace and sufficiency for every single thing I need. Amen.

13 - I Still Trust Him

"God is our refuge and strength, a very present help in trouble."

Psalm 46:1

AN EARTHLY SEASON is defined as a division of the year, marked by changes in weather, ecology, and hours of daylight. Earthly seasons result from the yearly revolution of the Earth around the Sun and the tilt of the Earth's axis relative to the plane of revolution. In temperate and polar regions, the seasons are marked by changes in the intensity of sunlight that reaches the Earth's surface, variations of which may cause animals to go into hibernation or to migrate, and plants to be dormant. As former Michiganders, we know about seasons because we had the privilege of living in a place where we experienced the beautiful distinctions of the seasons, sometimes experiencing winter, spring, summer, and fall all in one day.

The wisest man to ever live, King Solomon, also spoke of seasons, but with a biblical twist. Solomon said:

"To every thing there is a season, and a time to every purpose under the heaven: A time to be born, and a time to die; a time to plant, and a time to pluck up that which is planted; A time to kill, and a time to heal; a time to break down, and a time to build up; A time to weep, and a time to laugh; a time to mourn, and a time to dance" (Ecclesiastes 3:1-4).

Yes, it's obvious that King Solomon knew something from a biblical perspective about seasons. However, if we never read the dictionary to learn about the earthly definition of a season, and if, God forbid, we never read the Bible to learn about the biblical perspective on seasons, we would still be exposed to an experiential definition of life's seasons by virtue of walking through this existential situation called life. We can all testify that life is full of changing seasons. Yes, there are times:

- We laugh and times when we cry.
- When we have all the words to say, and times when we are left speechless.
- Things work out, and times when things fall apart.
- We can hear God, and times when, as hard as we pray, it seems the "open" light in heaven has been turned off.

And as we consider the changing seasons of life, an interesting interrogative arises:

How can you have stability in life when the seasons keep changing?

How can you celebrate God's grace while you're staring into a grave?

How can you be a champion in the middle of a crisis?

How can you live triumphantly in the middle of life's tragedies?

Beloved, I submit to you that it's possible to victoriously face the changing seasons of life. And the reason I know I'm right about it is because I know that God is still God, even in tough times. And when you know who God is, no matter what season of life you are facing, you can say with confidence, "I still trust Him!"

Have a look at the 46th number of the Hebrew hymn book of Psalms. The Psalms are nothing more than David's version of a gospel's greatest hits CD. When you read the psalms, it's like listening to one gospel jam after the next. This Hebrew hymn book has songs like Psalm 23:

"The Lord is my shepherd; I shall not want. He maketh me to lie down in green pastures: he leadeth me beside the still waters. He restoreth my soul: he leadeth me in the paths of righteousness for his name's sake. Yea, though I walk through the valley of the shadow of death, I will fear no evil: for thou art with me; thy rod and thy staff they comfort me."

Songs like Psalm 121:

"I will lift up mine eyes unto the hills, from whence cometh my help. My help cometh from the Lord, which made heaven and earth."

The Hebrew hymn book has jams like Psalm 34:

"I will bless the Lord at all times: his praise shall continually be in my mouth. My soul shall make her boast in the Lord: the humble shall hear thereof, and be glad. O magnify the Lord with me, and let us exalt his name together."

And in our text for consideration, we find David writing a song of trust to be sung by the sopranos, the Alamoth, while the sons of Korah were serving in the temple. And in this first verse we find 3 affirmations that encourage us to trust a God that can keep us during life's tough times.

1. God Is

First of all, David says, "God is..." And somebody reading this needs to know that God is an existential God. You can trust God because He lives. Watch the text. Of all the names of God David could have used, David uses the name Elohim. Elohim is a masculine plural noun, and if you know anything about the word plural, you know that means more than one. Some theologians suggest that this name of God speaks to the Trinity (Father, Son, and Holy Spirit). Elohim is the same name used in Genesis 1:1 where the record says, "In the beginning Elohim (Father, Son, and Holy Spirit) created ..." That means that there has never been a time when God was not. He's an existential God that will meet you wherever you live because He lives. I'm glad today that in this world of sometimes fake and fickle friends, in this capitalistic society where our children are taught to chase illusions of grandeur, in this world where people are dying—even being killed for senseless reasons—it's good to know a God that lives. I like the way this hymn puts it:

God sent His son, they called Him Jesus
He came to love, heal and forgive
He lived and died to buy my pardon
An empty grave is there to prove my savior lives
Because He lives, I can face tomorrow
Because He lives, all fear is gone
Because I know He holds the future
And life is worth the living, just because He lives

And can somebody take a moment and give Jesus a witness to testify that you know that God lives! You know that:

- You almost died, but you're alive today because He lives!
- You almost lost your house, but you're reading this book in your

living room because He lives!
- You almost lost your marriage, but you kissed your boo on their way to work this morning because He lives!
- Tough times had your talents tied up, but now you're making full view of the gifts God gave you because He lives!

He lives. He lives. He lives. You can trust our existential God because He lives!

2. God is Omnipotent

Not only does the text teach us that we can trust God because He is and always has been, but David also shows us that we can trust God because God is omnipotent. That is to say that you can have confidence in God because He is all-powerful. David says, "God is our refuge and strength." Joshua 20:3 notes that cities of refuge were places for people who unintentionally killed someone to run to for physical safety. And in these cities of refuge, the limitations set by the geographic boundaries would protect them from people that wanted to take them out.

However, in this psalm, David takes this concept a step further. David says that our limitless God Himself is the one that we can run to and we can know that His powerful arms are strong enough to keep us. And I don't know who I'm preaching to, but somebody reading this knows that there are times in life when we need to run to God's powerful arms. There are times when we need to run to God and be able to trust that He can keep us. Do you know that despite the circumstances of life, God is able to keep you? You see, even when solar power, horse power, human power has failed you, God still has power. God has ALL the power. God is so powerful that:
- He spoke and the world was created.
- He parted the Red Sea and the waters stood at attention as His people walked across on dry land.
- He stopped the sun so that Joshua could get his work done.
- When He speaks doors shut, and likewise, doors open.
- Paul said God is able to do, "exceeding abundantly above all that we ask or think, according to the power that worketh in us."

God's protection and strength knows no geographic, spiritual, mental, or emotional boundaries. You have to trust in that! I want to encourage you that you can trust our omnipotent God because He has all power!

3. God is Omnipresent

Not only does David show us that during the seasons of life we can trust God because He is existential, that is to say that He lives, and not only can we trust God because He is an omnipotent, all-powerful God, but lastly, the psalmist also teaches us that we can trust God because God is omnipresent.

We can have confidence in God because He is everywhere at all times. Watch the B portion of the text. David says, "God is a very present help in the time of trouble." Now the Hebrew word used here for trouble is *tsarah*. This word is found 73 times in the KJV Bible and every time it is used, it conveys the image of a tight place. What David is saying is that we can always depend on God to be with us, even when we find ourselves in a tight spot.

I know I've found myself in a tight spot. In those times I've found that my omnipresent God was there with me. I'm sure somebody reading this can say the same. And you know that God loved you so much that He refused to leave you there. He pried you out of that place, releasing you to live the best of your life. God will always outlast your troubles—and if you reach out to Him He can always be found because He is everywhere at all times.

"Well, preacher, how do I access Him?" you query.

I'm glad that you asked. All you have to do is believe in your heart and confess with your mouth.

"Well, preacher, what do I have to believe?"

Well, I'm glad you asked again. You've got believe the revelation of John 3:16 that, "God so loved the world, that he gave his only begotten Son, that whosoever believeth in him should not perish, but have everlasting life."

If you will trust your Savior, you ought to just bless yourself and say, in the words of Curtis Burrell, made famous by Rev. James Cleveland:

I don't feel no ways tired,
I've come too far from where I started from.
Nobody told me that the road would be easy,

I don't believe He brought me this far to leave me
Encourage yourself and say, "I still trust Him!"

Closing Prayer:

Almighty God, Elohim, I place my trust in Your power. I will run to You for refuge. I will not rely on the things in this world, which will one day fade away. Thank You for picking me up when I was in a tight place. Thank You for seeing me wherever I go because You are everywhere. This road is not easy, but I've got You, God, and for that I am eternally grateful. Amen.

14 - Anguish at the Cross

"And about the ninth hour Jesus cried with a loud voice, saying, Eli, Eli, lama sabachthani? that is to say, My God, My God, why hast thou forsaken me?"

Matthew 27:46

ANGUISH IS DEFINED as severe physical or mental pain and suffering. Synonyms for anguish include words like torture, torment, misery, sorrow, and heartache. As a matter of fact, God's servant Job, a man who knew a little something about mental and physical anguish, spoke of the reality of sorrow and suffering in Job chapter 14 verse 1 when he acknowledged that, "Man that is born of a woman is of few days and full of trouble." And brothers and sisters, as a child, I vividly remember one of my first introductions to anguish at a store that every child knows as Toys "R" Us. I remember it like it was yesterday. Mama loaded my brother and me into the car, and as soon as we pulled into the parking lot, we couldn't loosen our seat belts to make our mad dash into the store fast enough. You see, Toys "R" Us had a vast array of toys, so many toys in fact, that you could get lost. And on one fateful day I did just that, I wandered away from Mama. Oh she told me not to wander off, but I did. And I got lost. But I devised a plan in my 5 year old mind. I decided I would run as fast as I could from aisle to aisle, and that way I would be sure to find my mom. However, after sprinting up and down aisles 1-9 with no sign of her, I discovered that my strategy did not work. And, in my frustration, I leaned my back against a display of life-size Barbies and slid down to the floor. In my anguish, I found myself physically worn out, emotionally drained, and mentally exhausted.

And as I consider this experience that occurred on a lower, lesser, earthly level, I discovered a truth on a higher, holy, heavenly level, that there are times in this existential Toys "R" Us called life that you will find yourself physically worn out, emotionally drained, and mentally exhausted. Come on, you've been there before, you started off excited about runnin' through the TOY STORE of life, but then, LIFE HAPPENED and in an instant you got lost and found yourself experiencing torture, torment, misery, sorrow, heartache—or better yet, anguish. And in your frustration, after you had prayed and cried, and cried and prayed, you gave up, leaned your back against the Barbie display, and slid down to the floor trying to figure out how to get back to the One that brought you to this life in the first place.

Well, I want to encourage you to keep your eyes wide open because you will see the deliverance of the Lord in the land of the living. It's more than a notion that the same one who brought you 'to' is going to see you 'through.' In fact, I know that I know that I know that I know that the same one who strapped you in, the same one who turned the key in the ignition, the same one who carried you all this way will see you through. DO YOU KNOW THAT HE WILL SEE YOU THROUGH?

I really like the prophet Isaiah's declarative statement in chapter 64 verse 4. Isaiah said, "Since ancient times no one has heard, no ear has perceived, no eye has seen any God besides you, who acts on behalf of those who wait for him."

Then Paul remixed it and said it this way in 1 Corinthians 2:9, "No eye has seen, no ear has heard, no mind has conceived what God has prepared for those who love him."

Tell yourself, "I ain't seen nothing yet!" 'Cause some stuff starts happening when God has you on His mind. All of heaven is dispatched to address your situation when God has you in His mind. When you lift up your staff, waters are parted and you can walk on dry ground when God has you on His mind. And even in the middle of the storm, if God chooses to leave the water where it is, He will break the laws of physics and allow you to walk on the water when God has you on His mind.

Hear me: God is speaking a word to you in the middle of your anguish to let you know that HE HAS NOT FORGOTTEN YOU and Jesus has shown us how to handle our moments of anguish—down at the cross!

Go with me in your mind to the Matthean world of chapter 27.

Matthew records that the chief priest and elders, along with the high priest Caiaphas, plotted to kill Jesus. Consequently, in fulfillment of the prophetic texts, Jesus has been betrayed by one of his own. He's been scourged and mocked, and now Jesus hangs within an inch of his life on Golgotha's Hill.

Theologian Warren Wiersbe notes that, "Jesus was crucified at 9 o'clock in the morning; and from 9 until noon, He hung in the light. But at noon, a miraculous darkness covered the land. This was not a sandstorm or an eclipse, as some liberal writers have suggested. It was a heaven-sent darkness that lasted for three hours. It was as though all of creation was sympathizing with the Creator. There were three days of darkness in Egypt before Passover (Ex. 10:21–23); and there were three hours of darkness before the Lamb of God died for the sins of the world. Jesus had spoken at least three times before this darkness fell. While they were crucifying Him, He repeatedly prayed, 'Father, forgive them, for they know not what they do.' He had spoken to the repentant thief and assured him a place in paradise. He had also given His mother into the care of His beloved disciple, John. But when the darkness came, Jesus was silent for three hours."

After three hours, the darkness left. Then Jesus cried, "ELI, ELI, LAMA SABACHTHANI?" that is, "MY GOD, MY GOD, WHY HAVE YOU FORSAKEN ME?"

1. In your anguish, cry out to God

The first step in handling life's times of suffering, sorrow, and anguish is to understand that there will be circumstances in life that make you cry out to God! And y'all, if anybody had a right to cry out, it was Jesus. He'd:

done everything He was supposed to do,
helped everybody He was supposed to help,
went every place He was supposed to go,
loved everybody He could love,

And yet, here He is despised and dying between two criminals. That's enough to make anybody want to cry out. But we needn't look back over 2,000 years for a reason to cry out. Right here, live in our situation, we got enough to make us cry out:

Parents are killing children
People can't find jobs

Hard working people are losing homes
Our children are killing one another in the streets
HIV/AIDS is an epidemic in various communities

The devil has us so busy fighting one another that we've forgotten that he's the real enemy. That alone should be enough to make righteous indignation well up inside of you and make you want to cry out. And if I may say something parenthetically, this world does not benefit from your silence. There ought to be some injustices in our world, some injustices among God's people, that make you cry out! There will be times in this life when, in our anguish, we just need to cry out to God! Be real about right now!

2. Know Who you are crying to

Not only does Jesus show us that there are circumstances in life that make us want to cry out, but He also shows us that when we cry out, we need to know who we are crying to. Listen to the Hebrew writer, Matthew, in verse 46. Jesus says, "Eli, Eli." Immediately after Jesus said this, some people got it twisted and thought He was calling on the prophet Elijah. However, the Greek, Hebrew, and English translations show us that Jesus was calling on somebody we could all benefit from knowing and knowing better—God. You see, even as Jesus was momentarily forsaken by the Father as He took on the sins of the world, He kept hold of the Father as God. Christ was God's servant in the work of redemption so He calls Him God, for in His suffering He was doing His Father's will and this gave Him the resolve to hold fast to His purpose on the cross. And *that's* a word for somebody that's being hung up and hung out by the challenges of this life. You need to know that when you call on God, stuff begins to happen. You see, this wasn't just any old lil' 'g' God. This was big 'G' God—the one who theologian Anselm of Canterbury described in his ontological argument as, "a being than which nothing greater can be conceived." Jesus cried out to the God who:

- Sent His Son as the second Adam
- Changed the names of Abram and Jacob
- Had the power to consume Elijah's sacrifice
- Was David's war weapon against a Philistine giant named Goliath

This true and living God was the same One who, 33 years before, put Him in the womb of a virgin girl as a seed of salvation for all of humanity, just to get Him to this place in Matthew 27:46 to die for our sins and give us an opportunity to have eternal life.

Jesus was calling on the God who allowed a faith the size of a mustard seed to *make mountains commit suicide in the sea*, in the words of the late, great Dr. Gardner C. Taylor. When you get in the thick of life, when the going gets tough, when the funk hits the fan, you've got to know who to cry to! Look, it's alright to call on Mama, it's alright to call on Daddy, and it's alright to call on your friends, but you need to know who to call on first.

You see, when you have an emergency, when somebody's heart has stopped, you don't call your friend first and say, "Girl, you wouldn't believe what just happened, such-in-such's heart done stopped." No, the first thing you do is dial 9-1-1.

In the same way, when you have a situation in life that causes your heart to almost skip a beat, when you face something that almost levels you to the ground, the first thing you need to do is get down on your knees, put your hands together, and act like you know somebody who's bigger than your situation. In an emergency situation, you need to stretch your hands to God and cry out like you know He can and He will.

I know I can testify that there have been times in my life when I've done all I can do about a situation, there have been times when I've found myself concerned about the outcome and worrying about the income. I'm so glad that I had a mama and a daddy that taught me what to do at time times like that. You just need to go to your prayer closet and say:

Father, I stretch my hands to Thee,
No other help I know;
If Thou withdraw Thyself from me,
Ah! Whither shall I go?

Do you know Jesus is on the main line and all you gotta do is call Him up? Call Him up today and tell Him what you want. You've got to know who to cry to!

3. You need to know what to say

As Jesus hung on the cross that Good Friday night, our Savior teaches us that there are times we need to cry out to Him, and when we experience the anguish of life, we need to know who to cry to, but lastly, Jesus also teaches us that in our anguish we also need to know what to say. Somebody reading this needs to know, WHEN YOU CRY OUT, you need to know what YOU ARE SAYING!

Jesus says, "My God, My God, Why have you forsaken me?" Jesus is echoing part of a quote taken from the A portion of Psalm 22 verse 1 where David says the same thing. In Judaism, when a verse is cited, its entire context is implied. Important to note also is that Jesus is quoting a psalm that falls in the genre of laments. In Psalms of lament, the song writer cries out to God as honestly as possible about their current situation. In fact, the Jewish lament is not so much asking God "why" as it is simply being honest about the place they are so they can begin fresh and new. Simply said, we can better understand the Hebrew and Chaldean language Jesus speaks in verse 46 when we replace the mysterious question mark with an honest exclamation mark. In essence, Jesus is noting that this is not the end of the whole story, it's simply the conclusion of this part of it and the beginning of a new one.

I wonder how much better off we'd be if we replaced life's question marks with honest exclamations? You see, when you get to this point in your walk with the Lord, you'll go from asking, "Why did this happen?" to, "Lord, this happened, but I'm trusting you for this new beginning."

We go from, "Why did I lose the job?" to, "God, I know you to be a provider and every need shall be supplied."

We go from asking God, "Why don't I have a man or a woman?" to saying, "Lord I'm single, but I'm on your schedule."

"I don't know why they died, I don't know why I lost the house, but I do know that every time I say it the way it needs to be said, before my need gets out of my mouth, God is already working to supply every one of my needs."

I'm reminded of the story of one William Dixon. William Dixon lived in Brackenthwaite, England. He was a widower who had also lost his only son. One day he saw that the house of one of his neighbors was on fire. Although the aged owner was rescued, her orphaned grandson was trapped in the blaze. Dixon climbed an iron pipe on the side of the house and lowered the boy to safety. His hand that held on to the pipe was badly burned.

Shortly after the fire, the grandmother died. The townspeople wondered who would care for the boy. Two volunteers appeared before the town council. One was a father who had lost his son and wanted to adopt the orphan as his own. William Dixon was to speak next, but instead of saying anything he merely held up his scarred hand. When the vote was taken, the boy was given to him.

The reason you can handle life's sorrows is because Jesus has already paid the price with His scarred hands, and now we have an opportunity to be adopted into His family. I thank God for His scarred hands—hands that marched up a hill called Calvary. Hands that were nailed to an old rugged cross. Hands that hung limp when He died, but these same hands were raised in victory bright early on the third day morning.

Closing Prayer:

Father God. Thank You that You will never leave or forsake me. Thank You for sending Your one and only Son to die for my sins. God, when this life fills me with anguish, remind me who to cry out to. Remind me why I have the privilege of asking for Your help. Remind me who I belong to. Amen.

15 - Marred in His Hands

"The word which came to Jeremiah from the LORD saying, Arise, and go down to the potter's house, and there I will cause thee to hear my words. Then I went down to the potter's house, and, behold, he wrought a work on the wheels. And the vessel that he made of clay was marred in the hand of the potter: so he made it again another vessel, as seemed good to the potter to make it."

Jeremiah 18:1-4

OUR INTEREST IN this chapter is drawn to the concept of God using the imperfect substance of humanity to complete his perfect work.

In 1930, the East Lake community of Atlanta, Georgia was a popular vacation haven for Atlanta's well-to-do families. However, by the 1960s and 1970s this same community was all but illustrious and began to fall into despair; so much so that this area was labeled a war zone by local police because of its high crime rates and drug trade. However, in 1995, the East Lake Foundation was established to help transform the East Lake community and create new opportunities for the families who live there. The new East Lake community now includes a public golf course and a plethora of charter schools. The Foundation is beginning to break the cycle of poverty by creating and funding educational, recreational, and self-sufficiency programs using what already exists in the community to create something new; essentially recycling and rearranging the same substance.

I would suggest to you that if you find yourself in a state of confusion as you consider the mess that you've been through, and if you are locked up by the knowledge of what you anticipate to be a futile future filled with failure, there is a message of remaking and renewal echoing through 2,700 years of biblical history through the book of Jeremiah. If I could give you this entire sermon in a sentence I would tell you that although you might think you are nothing more than tarnished or blemished, you are made of something greater.

In the wailing prophet Jeremiah's time, Israel was no longer a unified nation. In the north, Israel had been destroyed and the people had been delivered into the hands of their enemies. Only Judah, the tribe that God would send the Messiah through, remained to the south. As one can imagine, this was a chaotic sociopolitical climate. In fact, everything surrounding the life and times of Jeremiah seems to maintain some type of confusion. Even the arrangement of the book itself lacks an identifiable order. In David A. Dorsey's article "Broken Potsherds at the Potter's House" (in the *Evangelical Journal*), he speaks of this puzzling phenomenon. Dorsey says that scholars can conclude that the book of Jeremiah in its present form "is in a state of inexplicable disarray."

Many of us are like the book of Jeremiah. On the outside we appear to have it all together, but on the inside our lives are in a state of inexplicable disarray. As Jeremiah walked the dusty, discouraging roads of Jerusalem, in the center of all this chaos, God prepared an observation for Jeremiah at a pottery near Jerusalem in the valley. The Hebrew word used in verse 2 means quite literally to "go down." This word is found 337 times in the KJV and every time it is used, a pivotal action follows. God essentially says, "Jeremiah, I've instructed you thus far to prophesy to a hard, obstinate people who have anything but a heart of flesh. Jeremiah, you know and I know that dealing with these church folk is not easy. At the Jerusalem Baptist Church, you've had to deal with many austere circumstances. Jeremiah, I need you to go on a retreat outside the city limits away from what you are used to. Go down to the potter's house because my people may be marred in my hand, but hope is not lost because they are made of my substance."

1. Marred in the Master's hands

In this solemn hour, I must confess that I have traveled with the Bible down to the potter's house and I discovered that if you are to experience reshaping in any aspect of your life, you have to know that you are marred in the hand of the potter. The language that Jeremiah uses suggests that there was a strange degree of imperfection about this clay. Something was not right about this clay. Verse four says that

Jeremiah discovered that the work that the potter was working so diligently on was "marred." It was battered, busted, broken, and disgusted.

Jeremiah probably observed this first because, much like the clay on the wheel at the potter's house, the sociopolitical situation outside the house was "marred" as well. Nevertheless, one thing was certain about the location of the clay—it was in the hands of the potter. As I consider this notion of reassurance because we are in God's hands, my mind goes back to the story of the sweet little five year old girl that stood on the corner of an empty Italian street, crying as she held her broken, battered, busted, and disgusted violin. It was then that a man walked out of a bakery on the corner and, noticing the little girl, said, "Little girl, why are you crying?"

With a trembling voice, the little girl replied, "I'm crying because my violin is broken."

The man took the violin from the little girl and she continued to cry. So, he asked again, "Little girl, why are you still crying? Don't you know who I am? I am the great violin maker Maggini and I've seen violins in this condition before. Leave it in my hands because I am able to fix it."

The potter knows something about mending broken pieces. The potter is a proficient professional in dealing with life's failures. The potter has experience with trying-and-failing and trying-and-failing. The Norwegian theologian Andreas Aarflot noted that God "can well endure our weakness as well as our success." You're not just messed up; you're messed up in the master's hands. I've got insurance with All-State and they reassure me that if anything happens I'm in good hands with them. But, I found out that if I don't pay the premium, those good hands are nowhere to be found. I'm glad that when I find myself deficient and lacking in the eyes of man, I can stand whole and complete before God because my life is in His hands. You may be marred, but you are in the hands of the potter!

2. Made of His substance

In the potter's hands you can be made again because you are made of His creative substance. God could have sent Jeremiah to the woodshop but, at best, a collection of saw dust could only be used to make flimsy unreliable particle board. However, stuff made of clay can be made again because it is made of a creative substance. God is...therefore, we are. That is tough for man to understand. This is the flexible substance that you are made of.

3. Able to be reworked

The latter part of verse four says that the potter took what he already had—that marred, blemished, broken, busted, and disgusted clay—and he made it again another vessel. I like how the New Oxford Annotated Bible words this verse. It says that the potter "reworked" the clay. This word rework implies some thoughtful intention on behalf of the potter. When I was a senior at San Antonio Cornerstone Christian School, I vividly remember choosing to enroll in an arts and crafts class to avoid having to suffer through a year of anatomy and physiology as an elective course. In this arts and crafts class we had the opportunity to work with red clay, or what was more properly termed, "terra cotta." I discovered that to prevent the clay from hardening overnight, I had to wrap it in moist paper towels so it would maintain its plasticity or ability to be molded. This gave me the ability to make it into something else at a later date.

However, I discovered something even more enlightening. I discovered that even if I left my unfinished work of clay out overnight and it hardened and dried up, all I had to do was grind what remained, add water, and I could make it into something else. Now, those techniques of preserving and reshaping clay helped me matriculate and make it through high school, but can I tell you something about preservation and reshaping that will usher you through life? When you find yourself left out in the overnight of life, if you have faith in the creative renewal of the potter's hands, He will wrap you in His moist towels of grace and mercy. Likewise, when you have stepped outside of God's grace and you feel dehydrated in your spirit, the process may hurt, but God will take and grind those experiences, add some moisturizing water, and rework you into another vessel.

If you were honest, you would testify that you've found yourself left out in the overnight of life. You've stepped outside of the umbrella of God's grace and found yourself exposed to some of the elements of life that God never intended. And now, when you look in the mirror, you no longer see the vibrant fluid person that you used to know but you see this old dried up dehydrated clay. Well, I've got good news for you fresh from the replenishing wells of Heaven. Child of God, don't get discouraged when you find yourself dried-up, dehydrated, and depleted because all it takes is for the potter to stop by, grind you in your dry state, add a little water to you, and shape you into what He wants you to be. Your appointment with adversity may just be God grinding you in your dry state so He can shape you into what He wants you to be. Friends, you are made of God's creative substance!

The Great Creator has the whole universe at His disposal, but all He desires is to mold the piece of Him that lives in you. Can you see my Jesus as the scribes and Pharisees are criticizing Him for the all-but-perfect disciples that he chose to be closest to him? I believe Jesus said, "My followers may be marred in My hands, but they are made of My substance." Can you see my Lord as those rusty nails are being driven into His innocent hands and feet and Satan whispering, "The same people that you lived for are killing you," and Jesus responding, "I'm not being murdered, rather, I freely give My life because My people may be marred in My hands, but they are made of My substance." Can you see my savior lying in that cold tomb as death and the grave are rejoicing for the battle they think they have won? However, the gospel writer tells me that He laid there on Friday night (as death mocked and scorned Him) and He laid there on Saturday night (as the grave ridiculed and disdained Him.) But early one Sunday morning He got up with the victory banner raised high for you and for me because He knew that we would be marred in His hands but made of His substance!

Closing Prayer:

Jesus, You gave Your life for undeserving me. I am ever-thankful that I am in the potter's hands. My creator holds me close and shapes me as He needs to. I willingly ask that You make me into that which You want me to be. Thank You, Jesus, that Satan won't win the battle for me. I trust You in all my ways. Amen.

16 - Directions in the Middle of a Mess-Up

"For the LORD will not forsake his people for his great name's sake: because it hath pleased the LORD to make you his people. Moreover as for me, God forbid that I should sin against the LORD in ceasing to pray for you: but I will teach you the good and the right way: Only fear the LORD and serve him in truth with all your heart: for consider how great things he hath done for you."

1 Samuel 12:22-24

EVERY FEBRUARY, AMERICA pauses to honor the invaluable contributions of African Americans. However, while watching the news one February morning, I witnessed a more sobering type of black history. A report was made of a young brother of ebony hue being killed right in my own community. As I listened, I tried to think of ways to describe how I felt. I thought, "Another piece of our future has died." But no, that conclusion would not do. I couldn't put my thoughts into words and finally I just declared, "You know, that's just messed up!" I tried to be more eloquent, but my right to be mad at the injustice in our society would ONLY allow me to say, "That's just messed up!" And while it is true that messed up stuff happens on a lower, lesser, earthly level, on a higher, holy, heavenly level, there will be times in your life when you will witness or be actively involved in some messed up stuff!

I believe I ought to have at least one witness reading this who knows what I'm talkin' about:

You've witnessed drugs in your community, or you've been actively involved with drugs—and the Spirit of the Lord has said to you, "That's messed up!"

You've seen the prisons swelling with men and women of color, or you've helped a prison swell and you've heard God say, "That's some messed up stuff!"

You've seen the breakdown of the nuclear family, or you've helped break a family down—and the One who sits high and looks low is saying, "That's messed up!"

Listen, wherever you find yourself on this continuum called life, whether you've been a witness or a participant, keep your faith in our communities, keep doing what you can to keep our people out of prison, keep believing in God's intent for the family, AND keep believing in the power of church participation because God is still God in the middle of a messed up situation.

The 12th chapter of First Samuel is bookended in a unique place. Chapter 11 details the glory of King Saul as he proves himself able to lead in battle against the Ammonites. And chapter 13 details the beginning of the story of Saul's reign as king. However, in chapter 12, situated between the glory and the story, is the "mess-up". Israel has asked for a king that God never intended for them to have. It is then that we find the prophet/judge Samuel at the twilight of his life, teaching the people how to live after they've messed up. And somewhere around verse 22 is where the rubber meets the road in our lives, because the prophet gives us some stuff we need to know before we learn what to do in the middle of a messed up situation:

1. God does not throw His people away. Israel is still God's chosen people even though they've messed up. If you know somebody that's made a mistake, don't you make the mistake of devaluing people who God values. You might be "done" with them, but God is not.
2. When you know somebody has messed up, pray for them and don't stop praying. We like to sing the song "You can depend on me to pray for you," but all we do is talk about folks. Prayer is power, and prayer changes things and people.
3. After you pray, do something. Don't leave folks hangin'. Go to God's word and instruct them in the way.

After verses 22 and 23, Samuel turns his attention to the place that we most often find ourselves, and he gives us some directions for when we find ourselves in the middle of a mess-up.

1. Place God in proper position

First of all, Samuel says in verse 24A, if you really want to get back on track after you've played a discordant note in the symphony of life, you've got to place God back in the proper position by fearing the Lord. In essence, he says, "Even though you have a man in front of you, don't forget the God above you."

Listen, you can't let the natural that you see override the supernatural that you can't see. And I've got to say this: don't you place the emotions and feelings in front of you, above the God that you serve. February is not only Black History month, it is also the month when Valentines are celebrated. Don't you let one day of celebrating a baby flying in a diaper with a bow-and-arrow cause you to make the mistake of acting married for one night.

Married folks, don't you let one argument cause you to start looking outside your covenant agreement. You've got to allow the God that you can't see to satisfy the needs that you can see. You've got to encourage yourself and say, "I can do it the way God said do it, even if I've never done it before." Keep God in His proper place by fearing the Lord!

2. Have a heart to serve God

Samuel's second direction for recovery in the middle of Israel's mess-up is found in the B portion of verse 24, where the prophet says, "serve him [God] in truth with all your heart." Samuel suggests that because God had a mind to save you, you ought to have a heart to serve Him. The Hebrew word used here for truth is *eh-meth*, which means faithfulness or stability. The people of Israel had messed up so badly by asking for a king, that this mistake could lead to their downfall if they didn't show God some stability or steadfastness in their service to Him. Likewise, the Hebrew word "serve" used here is found 294 times in the King James Version of the Bible. This is the same Hebrew word that was used in the Exodus narrative when God told Moses to go tell Pharaoh to let my people go so that they may serve me.

And at this point I've got to tell you, my brother or sister, that God didn't save you for saving's sake, God saved you for Kingdom service. So I guess the real question is what have you been doing since God picked you up? If you are saved, sanctified, and filled with the

Holy Spirit, what have you been doing since God turned you around? What have you been up to since God placed your feet on solid ground?

February is also the month in which the Super Bowl is played. When a coach wants to challenge a call, he throws a red flag onto the field. What would God see you doing if He threw a red flag and challenged what you claim has been taking place in your life? Would God go back to the replay booth and find you on the field of life playing or perpetrating? In this day and age, when:

- crime and violence is ravishing our communities,
- sexual deviance is the order of the day,
- we find ourselves lost on a carousel of contemporary concerns,

God needs some battle-tested soldiers who know they've been saved to serve. Your heavenly daddy needs some people with hearts that beat to the drum of the servant's National Anthem.

If I can help somebody as I pass along,
If I can cheer somebody with a word or song,
If I can show somebody he is trav'ling wrong,
Then my living shall not be in vain.

Listen, get off the bench, get back in shape, and get ready to get back into the game, because God saved you so that you can serve Him!

3. Consider what great things He has done for you

In the last portion of verse 24, Samuel concludes his encouragement by telling the people that it's easy to Fear the Lord, and Serve God faithfully when you "consider what great things He has done for you." What Samuel says here is one look back behind you ought to make you WANT to worship God in you.

No matter how much hell we've raised in our own lives, there's still some God in us. The problem in many instances is that we haven't slowed down long enough to see, with the eyes of our heart, how much God has kept us! We see in this text that the children of Israel had plenty to look back on. They could look back on the cloud by day, and the fire by night. They could look back on the God that split a Jordan River and brought down a Jericho River. The very fact that God was who He was for them and did what He'd done for them should make them worship Him!

The root of the Hebrew word used here for "done" literally

means to "twist," and as it is used here, it means to "make great." That means that every time you look back for yourself at how God twisted your situation and made Himself "greater than," it ought to make you want to worship HIM. Every time you realize, as John Claypool said, "God's power and willingness to forgive are greater than our human capacity to sin," you ought to want to worship Him. I don't know about you, but every time I think about:

1. JEHOVAH-JIREH... my provider
2. JEHOVAH-NISSI... the one who reigns in victory
3. JEHOVAH-SHALOM... my peace
4. JEHOVAH-TSID-KENU... my righteousness
5. JEHOVAH-SHAMMAH... the one who is everywhere at all times
6. JEHOVAH RAPHA... my healer

... my soul gets HAPPY! And I just want to worship Him. You see my testimony is a lot like yours:

Living, He loved me;
Dying, He saved me;
Buried, He carried my sins far away;
Rising, He justified freely forever;
One day He's coming—O glorious day!

God promised in 2 Chronicles 7:14, "If my people, which are called by my name, shall humble themselves, and pray, and seek my face, and turn from their wicked ways; then will I hear from heaven, and will forgive their sin, and will heal their land." Listen, God can use crooked lines to write straight. He can bless you smack in the middle of your mess-up.

Closing Prayer:

God, I am thankful today that You can take my mess-up and make it work out for Your glory and for my good. I humbly seek Your face in my trouble. In my distress I call out to You. Bring to mind areas I need to give over to You and bring that glorious healing to me today. Amen.

17 - What to Expect When You're Expecting

"Then said Mary unto the angel, How shall this be, seeing I know not a man? And the angel answered and said unto her, The Holy Ghost shall come upon thee, and the power of the Highest shall overshadow thee: therefore also that holy thing which shall be born of thee shall be called the Son of God."

Luke 1:34-35

THE WAY A baby is formed in the womb of a woman is one of the most amazing processes that God created. Think about it:
Month 1: A little embryo looks like a tadpole.
Month 2: The lil tadpole begins to look like a human and organ systems start developing.
Month 3: The mouth has 20 buds that will become teeth.
Month 4: The fetus moves and kicks.
Month 5: The fingernails grow.
Month 6: The eyes can open.
Month 7: The fetus can suck his or her thumb.
Month 8: The baby weighs about 5 pounds.
Months 9 and (possibly 10): Get the camera ready, because a baby is coming out!

What an amazing process! However, as awesome as this process is, there are a number of true stories of women carrying babies all the way from month 1 to month 9, all the way from an embryo to a baby, WITHOUT even knowing that they were pregnant. Let me see, how can I say this as Christian as possible? They were doing what it takes to *make* a baby with no expectation that they would actually *have* a baby! As I observed these stories in the natural, the Lord began to speak to me in the supernatural and said, "Some of my people don't even know that they're pregnant!"

So I said, "God, what do you mean?"

And the Holy Spirit said, "Maybe that was too heavy, let me say it this way: Some of my people have been doing what it takes for Me to move in a mighty way, HOWEVER I'm limited in doing anything because they don't expect anything to happen."

I said, "Whoa God, that's deep!"

But what is an expectation anyway? An expectation is a future-centered belief that something will happen. Let's do a real quick spiritual pregnancy test, because there might be somebody reading this who doesn't even know he or she is pregnant with the precious cargo of Calvary, called the message of Jesus Christ. Here's how you do a spiritual pregnancy test: Put your hand on yourself. Now, if you're still here AND you got strength in your body, if you've got clapping in your hands and stomping in your feet, if you've got a little piece of mind left, well then, God ain't through with you yet and YOU ARE PREGNANT!

- God's about to kick something off in your life like you've never seen before.
- God's about to give birth to something in you like you've never seen before.
- God's about mend a broken heart, set the captive free.
- God's about to open blind eyes, make the deaf to hear, and the mute to speak.
- God's about to turn pimps and prostitutes into preachers and prophets.
- God's about to take the weak and make them strong.
- God's about to take the poor and make them rich in Christ Jesus.

As a matter of fact, if you don't remember anything else you read in this chapter, remember that God will demonstrate the Holy Spirit working in your life. But the question remains: "What do you expect now that you are expecting?" The disciple Luke provides us with an answer to this question here in the first chapter of Luke. And you know who Luke is don't you? Luke is the Syrian physician from Antioch credited with writing this book and the book of Acts. He's the one who arguably emphasizes Jesus's Jewish roots and the power of the Holy Spirit more so than any other gospel writer.

And in this first chapter, Luke tells how the angel Gabriel has gone to Mary's brother in-law Zechariah and pronounced the birth of Jesus's cousin, John the Baptist. And in our focal passage (Luke 1:34-35), this same angel, Gabriel, was sent by God to the little town of Nazareth to deliver a special message to a teenaged Jewish virgin girl named Mary. In essence, this angel was sent by God to an unusual place, with a unique message, for an unsuspecting person. When God sends a special agent to an unusual place, with a unique message, for an unsuspecting person or people, that means something special is about to happen. OK, you don't believe me?

Come here, Noah, tell this reader how God told you to build a boat when no rain had ever fallen. Tell us how, in faith, you built the boat, rain came, and your family was saved because you knew something special was about to happen.

Come here, Abraham, tell God's child how God told you to go to a far place and you went and became the father of many nations... all because you knew something special was about to happen.

Come here, Paul, tell my brother or sister about the Damascus road and how God knocked you down and changed your life... all because something special was about to happen.

All I'm trying to say is when God sends a special agent to an unusual place, with an unusual message, for an unsuspecting people... something special is getting ready to happen!

So the angel Gabriel goes and says, "Mary, not because of anything that you've done, but because God is God, He's favored you and you are going to be the mother of the Messiah, the one the Old Testament was looking forward to and the one the New Testament looks back at and waits for."

Mary's response to the angel is what we need to see. When you are expecting God to birth something in your life...

1. You've got to ask the right questions

It's amazing to me that after all the angel has pronounced, Mary, a devout church-going girl, still had questions. Look at the proclamations the angel makes in verses 30-33. He says:

- You've found favor with God.

- You will conceive and bear a son.
- You will name him Jesus.
- He will be great and be called the Son of the Most High.

However, after all of this, it seemed that Mary still had a question. Mary says, "How shall this be, seeing I know not a man?" The phrase "to know" here is another way of expressing sexual involvement. Mary says, "I'm a good Jewish girl and I ain't gettin' down like that. You got some explaining to do because I DON'T KNOW A MAN!"

It seems here that Mary doubts what God has said through this angel, just like her brother in-law Zechariah doubted earlier in the chapter. However, when we look deeper, we see that Mary was not doubting, she simply wanted to go deeper in her understanding of what was about to take place by asking the right questions. You see, Zechariah was looking for a sign on which to base his faith, while Mary went deeper in her faith to understand this sign. Mary believed the promise, but she knew she needed to go deeper to understand how this thing would be performed. And you need to know that it's not important that you always know what God is doing, as long are you are willing to go deeper. The Spirit of the Lord is saying that it's time to ask the right questions. It's time to go deeper. It's time to:

- Love God like you've never loved God before.
- Go to church like you've never gone to church before.
- Give of your time, talent, and treasure to the church like you've never given before.
- Embrace the vision like you've never embraced it before.
- Encourage somebody like you've never encouraged somebody before.

The reality is you can't get somewhere you've never been IF you're not willing to go somewhere you've never gone. It makes no sense for you to pray, "God, enlarge my territory," if you know you don't plan on coming out of your comfort zone.

I can remember when I was a child, we'd be at the city pool wading in the shallow end. And one day, my cousin wised up and blew my mind. He said, "I don't know why we're down here in the shallow end when we all know how to swim."

And that's my word for you today—take the floaties off and go down to the deep end. The deep end is where lives are being changed day-after-day. The deep end is where sanctuaries are filled during weekly Bible study. The deep end is where the enemy is bowing down at the feet of Jesus. The deep end is where the Holy Spirit fills the place so much that all we can do is lift our hands and worship!

Sometimes you have to tell the folks around you, "Move outta' my way... I'm goin' deep!" You've got to ask the right questions!

2. Expect God to do what only God can do

Not only does the Apostle Luke show us that when we expect God to move in a mighty way we've got to ask the right questions, but he also shows us that we can expect God to do what only God can do. You can do some great stuff by yourself, but there are seasons of your life when only God can do it. Listen to what the angel says in verse 35 section A. Gabriel says, "The Holy Ghost shall come upon you and the power of the Highest shall overshadow thee."

The Greek phrases used here for "come upon" and "overshadow" literally mean to "rest on" and "envelope in a haze of brilliancy." It's the same language used to describe the Shekinah glory of God that rested in the Old Testament Temple like a thick smoke when true worship was taking place. The angel Gabriel is saying to Mary, "Mary, the glory of God is going to cover you so much so that you're not going to have to do anything but keep yourself enveloped in it." You see, God didn't need a man AND a woman to make this AMAZING thing happen. ALL he needed was Mary to humble herself and surrender to his glory! Just take a look at Mary's resume and I believe she'll testify that it was nobody but the Lord.

Listen, you've been struggling long enough, just surrender to God's glory! Sometimes, God has to snatch control out of your hands so you don't end up with the wrong testimony. And you do know that it's possible to end up with the wrong testimony. The wrong testimony says, "I made it all by myself." The right testimony says, "I know it was nobody but the Lord!" God wants your testimony to be like Mary's, who said, "I know it was nobody but the Lord!"

Your education? Experience? Special skills? References? Food on the table? Clothes on your back? It was nobody but the Lord! Expect God to do what only God can do.

3. Expect your blessing to look like God did it

And when you go deeper with the Lord in your faith and you let God do what only God can do, you can expect that which you birth to look like the One who allowed you to birth it. At the end of verse 35, Gabriel says, "The holy thing that will be born of you shall be called the Son of God."

It's interesting that the angel says it "shall" be, and not, it "might" be called the Son of God. That's because, when God is all up in it, make no mistake about it, it's going to look like God. And I don't know about you, but I don't want it if it doesn't look like God. I just don't want it. I want to know for sure that this one came from God! But how can you know it came from God? Because it's going to love like God. You'll know it's from God because:

It's going to give far more than it takes like God.
It's going to bless your life like God.
It's going to create like God.

I remember when I was a child going to our annual summer family reunion in El Dorado, Arkansas. I'd be walking at the family picnic and my younger, distanced cousins would always ask, "Who are your kinfolk?" They didn't even know we were cousins. However, there was always a group of seniors who sat in the shaded area by the pecan trees who would stop me, look me up and down, and say, "You gotta be Bubba's baby boy, cause you look just like yo' daddy."

If you have any doubt that this move of the Spirit sweeping over your life is from the Lord... just grab it by the shoulders and look it up and down, cause I can guarantee you... it looks just like OUR DADDY! You can embrace this joy because it looks like the one it came from. You can clap your hands and you can stomp your feet and celebrate this mighty move of God because it don't look like me, and it don't look like you... it looks just like the One it came from! It looks just like our Daddy! You can know what to expect when you're expecting!

Closing Prayer:

Daddy, Thank You that I can expect You to move mightily in my life. Thank You that the things You bring into my life will reflect Your Shekinah Glory. I place it all into Your hands and I will wait expectantly for You to bring it to fruition at the right time. Amen.

18 - I'm Moving Forward

"Then we turned, and took our journey into the wilderness by the way of the Red sea, as the LORD spake unto me: and we compassed mount Seir many days. And the LORD spake unto me, saying, Ye have compassed this mountain long enough: turn you northward."

Deuteronomy 2:1-3

A FEW YEARS ago I was watching Good Morning America and the story of little Cheyenne Leslie was reported. Looking at this energetic four year old, one would say that Cheyenne was like any other preschooler. However, Cheyenne had a debilitating problem; Cheyenne has cerebral palsy, and just the year before was unable to take 2 steps without falling. In September of 2007, as she and her grandmother waved goodbye to her mother who was leaving to serve our country in Iraq, Cheyenne committed in her lil' heart that when her mother got back home, she would no longer be using her walker, but she would run into her mother's arms. And it made me think that sometimes we, too, find ourselves in a Cheyenne situation; a situation where:

- You had to face some things beyond your control.
- You had to look beyond your own strength and reach for a higher strength.
- You realized that doing the same thing the same way keeps getting you the same results.

Well, let me encourage you, brothers and sisters. Don't you lose sight of the finish line and don't you let go of the purpose that God has created you for. In our text for study in this chapter, you will see that God is calling you to move forward.

Live on the scene in this text, Moses is leading the transition of God's people from slavery in Egypt to the Promised Land in Canaan.

God had just delivered His people with a mighty hand from the shackles of bondage in Egypt; He had opened the Red Sea and fanned the bottom so that His people could walk across safely on dry land. After they had crossed the sea, God proved Himself to be Jehovah-Jireh, their provider, as He guided them with a cloud by day and a pillar of fire by night. He even provided some hot-water cornbread and fried chicken (ALSO KNOWN AS manna and quail) to eat. While logic would suggest that God's people had been provided with everything they needed to move forward, the Bible says that these people were not found advancing, but had been walking around the same mountain for a long time. In fact, it had been "many days." The "many days" described by the text equates this time as 38 years. It had been thirty-eight long, hot years with no ice water or A/C, and these people were moving nowhere fast. Their lack of obedience to God's divine plan left them literally walking around the blessing that had been promised to them years ago! They stood on the premises without God's permission to lay hold of the promises He made to them. However, on this particular day, God remembered those promises and the time had come to stop moving in circles and move toward a new future.

1. God has given the message

The first thing this text is tailored to teach us is that God has given you the message to move forward. In the text, God's people were not operating anywhere near their full potential as it related to their commitment to Him. And, don't you know that when you are living below your full level of potential God knows how to get your attention. Take a look at the Hebrew words Moses uses in verses 1 and 2 to describe when God "spoke" to him. In verse 1, Moses uses the general Hebrew term for "spoke" when describing God's instruction for the people to return to the wilderness. However, in verse 2 Moses uses a Hebrew term to describe when God "spoke" that is typically used when a situation is about to go in a new direction. From a literary stand-point you could stop at verse 2 and not read the rest of the story but know the ending of the story because of the difference in that one word.

Wrapped in the difference of one word is the same message, "Move forward." Isn't that just like God... that all it takes to make a difference is one word? I believe that someone can testify that you were smack dab in the middle of some mess, and you listened to the advice of so-called friends, but their words proved powerless. Then God came along and said the same word a different way and you watched your situation change before your very own eyes.

There you were, you had prayed all day and all night with tears flowing down your face, but all it took was one word and you lifted your eyes to the hills and you were able to stop telling God how big the problem was and you began telling the problem how BIG your God IS. If you don't believe me, let me call a witness to the stand.

Come here, Job; tell this reader how you had lost everything and you were in the fight of your life. You listened to the words of man, but their words proved powerless. Job, tell them all it took was one word from the Lord and you knew restoration was on the way.

Come here, Moses; jump out of the Old Testament and tell my friends how your stuttering words proved powerless before mighty pharaoh, but you steadied your tongue long enough to tell this earthly king, "I AM sent me. You better let my people go," and suddenly chains were broken and people were set free.

On the heels of those two testimonies I've just got one question for you: Do you really want to be set free by God's message to move forward? Would you be bold and say right now to God, "Lord this message to move from where I am to where I need to be includes me!"

When you understand the power of the moment that God speaks change into your life, then you know that you are included in His message to move forward. Then you can say, "Ain't no doubt about it. God has given me the message to move forward!"

2. God has given the means

Not only has God given you the message to move forward, but God has given you the means to move forward. The means to move forward answers the question, "Now that I know God is committed to the promise He made to me a long time ago, what do I have in my possession that will help me move forward?" Friend, be encouraged that God has given you what you need to move forward.

The Bible says that after 38 years in the wilderness, the people still existed. Over the years, many people had died walking around the mountain, but there were many that were still alive. What Moses is implying is that God gave them His unmerited favor; God gave them grace as a means of moving forward and this grace was manifested by the fact that they were still alive. When a person works an eight-hour day and receives a fair day's pay for his or her time, that is called a wage. When a person competes with an opponent and receives a trophy for his or her performance, that is called a prize. When a person receives recognition for high achievements, he or she receives an award. But when a person is not capable of earning a wage, can win no prize, and deserves no award—yet receives such a gift anyway—that is a good picture of God's unmerited favor.

You may have been through some things last year, but by the grace of God you are still here. That may not mean anything to some of you, but live a little while and have your life and your livelihood threatened, have your character and your reputation drug through the mud, lose a close friend to the same foolishness that you used to engage in, and you will be driven to your knees where you will thank God that you are still here. Sometimes we approach life with an arrogance that can only be matched by arrogance itself. You are not still kickin' because your alarm clock woke you up. You are not alive because you are such a good person. If you think otherwise, then let me tell you, I've been invited to more funerals than I care to count this year alone. And they were all good people! You are not at this particular place at this particular time on accident; you made it when no one else did because God in His sovereign grace and mercy has you here on assignment.

You may have done some things for which you have never forgiven yourself. Stop circling your mountain of despair and show yourself the same grace that God has shown you. YOU ARE STILL HERE!

- You may not have everything you used to have, but you're still here.
- You may not be who you used to be, but you are still here.
- You may not have done what you should have done, but you are still here.
- You're holding on to a broken piece, but you are still here.
- You may have to do some stuff over, you may have to do some stuff differently, you might have to earn some people's trust back, but you are still here!

In spite of what you've been told, there is power in your presence. In fact, your life is worth God giving His Son. God has given you grace as a means of moving forward!

3. God has given the motivation

Not only has God given you the message and the means to move forward, but God has also given you the motivation to move forward. You can hear the message to change your life. You can have the means to change your life, but without the motivation to move, you aren't going anywhere. It's easy to get accustomed to an unproductive job, it's easy to get used to an unproductive marriage. It's even easy to get used to an unproductive church if you lack motivation.

After 38 years of circling the mountain and going nowhere, one would think that the opportunity to move forward would be long gone. As you can imagine, the Israelites' camp was probably an experienced psychologist's nightmare. Here you had thousands of people who had lost their will to engage in a progressive productive lifestyle because they thought they had no reason to do so. What reason did they have to move forward? From their perspective, Moses didn't know what they had been through in Egypt. He wasn't there when they were being taken advantage of. He wasn't there when they were called "Hebrews" instead of "the children of Israel." Moses wasn't there when the dust from chiseling rocks all day threatened to suffocate them. Their unique experience of bondage declared that they had a right to stay right where they were. If their marriages failed, if their children fell by the wayside, if modern genocide persisted, if brothers killing brothers persisted, then they had a right to stand around and do nothing about their circumstance because *nobody* knew where they were from and what they had been through. It would seem as though they had a civil right to lack motivation.

However, when the Lord spoke in verse 3 He said, "You have circled this mountain long enough." This was a declaration that the opportunity for a new future still existed. The opportunity was still knocking. While Moses could not feel them, God could. The motivation to move forward was the fact that after all of life's challenges the opportunity to do better still existed. And I don't know about you but I get excited and feel a refreshed motivation when I think about the fact that after all I have been through, after all that people put me through, after all that I've put myself through, the opportunity still exists.

You might be saying within yourself, "Preacher, you don't know my struggle. You don't know my story. You don't know about my pain, the silence, and the isolation."

Well let me be the first to admit: I don't know. However, I do serve a God who does know. He's heard your cry. As a matter of fact, when you cried, He cried. He sent me to tell you to move forward because your hopes and dreams still exist. Your motivation lies in the fact that the opportunity is still alive! It's not over yet! It's still alive!

When Cheyenne's grandma learned that Cheyenne's mama was on her way back from Iraq, they went to meet her at the airport. As soon as Cheyenne saw her mama, she got nervous and wondered if she'd fall BUT then she thought about:

- All the physical therapy she'd been through,
- All the times she fell and got back up again,
- All the people that she had in her corner,

She said to herself, in spite of my condition, I can make it! I'm movin' forward! And she ran into her mama's arms. When you are in a situation that makes your legs shake and you wonder if you can make it, remember your spiritual therapy. Think about the God who picks you up and turns you around. And then declare, "I'm moving forward!"

Closing Prayer:

Lord, may I never stay still when You've given me the command to move forward. Thank You for the message, the means, and the motivation. Give my legs God-strength to move when You say, "Move!" Thank You for dying on the cross that I may have life in these bones and the breath in my lungs to do Your will. Amen.

19 - Weep No More

"But I would not have you to be ignorant, brethren, concerning them which are asleep, that ye sorrow not, even as others which have no hope. For if we believe that Jesus died and rose again, even so them also which sleep in Jesus will God bring with him. For this we say unto you by the word of the Lord, that we which are alive and remain unto the coming of the Lord shall not prevent them which are asleep. For the Lord himself shall descend from heaven with a shout, with the voice of the archangel, and with the trump of God: and the dead in Christ shall rise first: Then we which are alive and remain shall be caught up together with them in the clouds, to meet the Lord in the air: and so shall we ever be with the Lord. Wherefore comfort one another with these words."

1 Thessalonians 4:13-18

THE LATE, GREAT, African American poet James Weldon Johnson's sermon, "Weep No More," is a powerful portrayal of death. He describes God giving command to an angel to summon Death to His throne. God commands Death to bring "Sister Caroline" to Him. Soon, the poetic scene transitions to an image of Sister Caroline being rocked in the bosom of Jesus. As the angels sing in unison, the Savior wipes away her tears and uses His reassuring hand to smooth the furrows of pain from her face. In this single loving act, the family of Sister Caroline is reminded again that the hand in sovereign control of all things has given them an everlasting reason to 'weep no more.'

This illustrative poem reminds me that even when you know Christ, even when you have a thriving relationship with the Savior, sad situations will surface that will cause you to weep. The stark reality of being a normal human being, living a normal human life, is that abnormal situations will arise. There have been and will be times when the opportunity will arise—and times when the opportunity will fade away. There will be times when the door will open—and times when, as hard as we try to hold it open, the door will close. And no matter what, you need to know that God is well able to handle lost opportunities, and MY God is well able to strengthen you when doors have been closed. And like the saints of old used to say, in the sweet bye and bye, God will give you an everlasting reason to weep no more!

Like James Weldon Johnson's poetic sermon, our scripture passage for examination also finds a poet/prophet encouraging his generation to weep no more. During Paul's mission to Athens, Greece, he had sent Timothy to Thessalonica to encourage them and bring back a detailed report of their condition. Although there was much to be encouraged about, one issue was of grave concern. Some members of the newly formed congregation had died. The common belief was that all Christians would physically live to experience the return of Christ. With this belief in mind, the Thessalonian believers were concerned that those believers who had already died would miss the return of Christ and be lost for all eternity. Paul stops short of entering a doctrinal discussion about "what happens when we die," and instead, provides some much needed practical pastoral care by reminding them of the articles of their faith. Pastor Paul assures them that those who had died in Christ would be caught up to meet the Lord just like those who are alive at His coming. There are a couple of things I'd like you to store into memory about this passage to remind yourself in those difficult moments to weep no more.

1. We grieve differently

Christ followers do not grieve as others do. Look at verse 13. Paul reassures us that even though we will grieve, we grieve with HOPE. Paul does not offer them the comfort that "death is natural" or that "death is inevitable" and their loved ones "no longer suffer." No, no, Paul recognizes that this community is grieving in a real way; as Jesus did when Lazarus died, but they grieve in a way that is different from non-believers. They grieve in the way the Christian community grieves; with the Greek *elpis*, hope or expectation.

When the storms of life arise, when the kitchen gets hot, and when the goin' gets tough—you can't afford to forget about the hope you have in Christ. You can't afford to forget that:

- Weepin' may endure for the night, but joy comes in the morning.
- There's a Balm in Gilead to heal your soul.
- There is victory in Jesus!

You can sing the chorus to this old hymn ("Never Alone") to affirm your hope in Christ:

No, never alone.
No, never alone.
He promised never to leave me,
Never to leave me alone.

You can make the decision right now that you're going to grieve this loss, but you don't have to grieve like the hopeless because your hope is in Christ!

2. Our hope is built on the resurrection

Not only does Paul note that Christians grieve with hope, but he notes in verse 14 that this hope is built on the resurrection of Jesus Christ. Friend, you need to have a HOPE built on a Jesus who's been raised from Joseph's borrowed tomb. You see, the reality is that there are a lot of people who have misappropriated their hope. They've put hope in houses, they've put hope in land and they've put their hope in other people, but Paul notes that if we believe that the cross is still vacant, the tomb is still empty, and Jesus is still at the right hand of our Father's throne, then our hope is in the right place. Paul understands Jesus's resurrection to be the first step in the final triumph of God. That's why Paul was able to know with confidence in verses 16 and 17 that:

The Lord himself shall descend from heaven with a shout, with the voice of the archangel, and with the trump of God: and the dead in Christ shall rise first: Then we which are alive and remain shall be caught up together with them in the clouds, to meet the Lord in the air: and so shall we ever be with the Lord.

In times like these, we need to pause and reaffirm our hope in Christ's resurrection. We need to pause and reaffirm that Jesus was:

- Revealed in the flesh
- Vindicated in the spirit

- Seen by the angels
- Proclaimed by the Gentiles
- Put to death on an old rugged cross
- Placed in a borrowed tomb
- Raised on the 3rd day morning

AND He's comin' back again for all who believe!

I don't know about you, but I'm standing with the hymn writer who said,

My hope is built on nothing less,
Than Jesus' blood and righteousness.
I dare not trust the sweetest frame,
But wholly lean on Jesus' name.
On Christ the solid rock I stand,
All other ground is sinking sand.
All other ground is sinking sand.

Weep no more.

Closing Prayer:

Jesus, my desire is to know just like Paul did that grieving in this world, although a guarantee, is different from the grief of those who don't know You. Lord, when I must grieve, let me be filled with the hope that You have defeated death once for all eternity. Let my hope rest in Your resurrection and the confidence that You are LORD over all that is seen and unseen. Praise You, Jesus. Amen.

20 - Making a Choice to Live Chosen

"For he established a testimony in Jacob, and appointed a law in Israel, which he commanded our fathers, that they should make them known to their children: That the generation to come might know them, even the children which should be born; who should arise and declare them to their children: That they might set their hope in God, and not forget the works of God, but keep his commandments: And might not be as their fathers, a stubborn and rebellious generation; a generation that set not their heart aright, and whose spirit was not stedfast with God."

Psalm 78:5-8

WITH ALL THAT'S going on in the world, I find myself watching more and more of the daily news. A few months ago, I saw a crazy story about a man from California. The news reported that many Californians had been given ample time and opportunity to leave before a storm from the Pacific Ocean reached the west coast. Nevertheless, as strange as it sounds, one man was determined to brave the violent storm and stand on the beach so that he could take pictures of what he considered to be a 'rare natural wonder.' Sadly, the news also reported that this man made a fateful decision to take these pictures, as he was swept away and drowned by the storm, never to be seen again. As you're reading this story you're probably thinking, "What person in his or her right mind would stand on the beach taking pictures while a storm is approaching?" To be honest with you, I thought the same thing. However, I beg you to consider his actions from a higher, holy, heavenly perspective. Why is it that we too stand on the shores of our existence, admiring the temporal things of life, even while deadly storms are approaching? Think about it, we engage the very same things that we have seen destroy lives around us. So very often we find ourselves being swept away by the usual suspects of life:

- Yes, we know our finances can't handle that big purchase, but we buy it anyway and are swept away by a sea of bills.
- Yes, God showed us that he or she wasn't good for us, but we get with them anyway and find ourselves swept away by heartbreak after heartbreak.
- We drink or we smoke, knowing full well it's bad for us, but what do we do? We do it anyway and are swept away by storms of addiction.

One definition of insanity is to do the same thing repeatedly, expecting different results. Thanks be to God that He is still faithful, even when we're foolish. Our poor choices are no match for the grace of God. Look, I know some things have messed you up in the past, but today is the day you can make a choice to live stronger, wiser, and better. As a matter of fact, if you don't remember anything else, remember this: You are chosen of God and you have everything inside you to make a choice to live chosen.

In the text of Psalm 78 we find the psalmist addressing folks like you and I, folks that had some issues. The song writer is reviewing Israel's history, particularly, their 40 long years in the wilderness. By reviewing Israel's history, the psalmist wants the current generation to know and remember that God has done great things in the past, and if they will make choices that please God, He will continue to do great things in the future. Friend, in case you forgot, God is able to bless you tomorrow, just like He did yesterday. I don't know who I'm speaking to, but you serve a God of the encore, and if you call on Him in His will, He's able to come back out on the stage of your life and do what He did for you yesterday, all over again. The psalmist had to say this because the people had a history of forgetting what God had done and they needed to be reminded of what they were made of and the character of the true and living God they served. The whole of this psalm seeks to justify why God chose Judah as His chosen tribe and that stone-totin', giant-slayin' David as king. The psalmist notes that God has chosen Israel, but they have to make a choice to live like chosen people.

In verses 7 and 8, the psalmist uses an ancient literary method called synonymous and antithetical parallelism. Now don't get lost in those big words, it just means in one verse he shows what God wants us to do now and in the other verse he shows what God doesn't want us to do. In verse 7 the psalmist says that if you are going to make a choice to live chosen:

1. You have to choose to set your hope in God

In essence, you must place all your confidence in God. I'm not lying to you, look at the Hebrew words in verse 7. The Hebrew words used here are unique. Of the many names of God the psalmist could have used, he uses the name Elohim, the personal name of God used when referring to the one big 'g' God above all the other little 'g' gods. He also uses the Hebrew word for hope that literally refers to the loin of an animal, the area called the leaf fat. Now, leaf fat is the area around the kidneys of an animal that has the highest concentration of fatty tissue. This part is ideal for baking and frying because it's high in saturated fat and it doesn't have any flavor from the animal in it, it's just fat. What the writer is saying here is if you want to live as a chosen person, you have to deliberately cast the highest concentration of your abilities, resources, time, energy, and substance above all these little 'g' gods. The writer says, "Look no further than the 1st part of verse 8 to find out what people look like whose hopes are in all the wrong places."

The folks in Israel's past were known as stiff-necked people. In fact, there was nothing more remarkable about their early history than the fact that God couldn't bless them because they wouldn't fully trust Him. And at this point I've got to ask you, "Is that all you want said about you? That God couldn't bless you to the utmost because you couldn't trust him to the fullest?" You've got to trust the plan God gives, even when you cannot trace how He's getting it done. When you allow yourself to get to this place in your faith walk, then you'll be able to say;

- Bills have one more day to be paid, but I still trust Him.
- Still havin' difficulty at school, but I still trust Him.
- I'm afraid to die and afraid to live, but I still trust Him.
- Wish I had a little bit more, but I still trust Him.

You ought to just take a prophetic moment and serve notice to your circumstances and tell God, "If You did it before, I trust in Your will that You can do it again! God, I need an encore! God, I'm standin' in the need, I still trust You, I still believe. I'm yet holdin' on! Lord, I'm trusting You to do what You did last time all over again!"

You've got to get a theology like that old cornflakes commercial. Remember it? The adult tastes the cornflakes, loves them, and at the end the slogan goes, "Taste them again, for the first time."

Can you trust that God will allow you to taste His goodness for the first time all over again? If you believe it today, you ought to straighten your back, square your justified shoulders, and choose to set your hope in God!

2. You have to do what God says

The psalmist goes on to show in verse 7 that as God's chosen people, we must choose to keep God's commandments. Essentially, the only way you can look forward to God's salvation is by doing what God says. The Hebrew word used here implies the deliberate preservation of what God has ordered us to do. Through the recitation or reading of this psalm in corporate worship, the song writer is calling all people who profess relation to Israel to relationship with God. And listen, there is a difference between being related to something and having relationship with it. When you acknowledge that you are related to someone, you are simply making note of a logical, static connection. But, when you intentionally acknowledge a relationship, you are acknowledging an interpersonal association. When you're related you're just part of the crowd, but when you're in right relationship things happen.

God desires for you to experience the wonderful joys of life and life more abundantly. There are things that God wants to jump off for you in your life, but He can't do it without your permission. And the way you give God permission to bless you abundantly is by having an active relationship with Him. You never really know how God will bless you when you choose to keep God's commandments.

3. You have to choose to remember what God has done

Lastly, the songwriter shows us that if we are going to really live as champions of choice, we have to choose to remember what God has done. Theologian C.H. Spurgeon once said, "He who does not keep

God's love in memory is not likely to keep His law." The fact of the matter is you have to do some things on a daily basis to remind yourself of what God has done. Instead of just waking up in the morning with your mind stayed on Jesus, spend some intentional devotional time in His word, centering your thoughts on the greatness of God and His activity through you.

In verse 7, the writer reminds us not to forget the works of God. The psalmist is not referring to the works of God in creation. He is pointing Israel's memory toward what God has done in administering His government over mankind. Remembering what God has done for you and those around you is no small thing to God. Look at verse 11. Ephraim was once God's chosen tribe, but because of their apparent penchant for memory loss, God rejected them and chose Judah. The hymn writer says, Israel, don't you forget how God:

- Parted the Red Sea and closed it up on Pharaoh's army.
- Led you with a cloud by day and a pillar of fire by night.
- Fed you with fried quail and hot water cornbread, better known as manna.
- Told Moses, "You've been traveling around this mountain long enough, and it's time to head toward the Promised Land."
- Blessed you back then and He's still blessing you right now.

Now, let me let you in on something... You have to be familiar with something before you can remember it. You have to know it before you can recall it. I know you know the Lord has been good to you. When I think about the goodness of the Lord and all that He's done for me, I just lose myself and shout, "Hallelujah!" Thank You, God, for the ability to remember how good You've been. How You put food on my table, clothes on my back, and made a way out of no way.

When the doctors said I shouldn't even be here, Mama and Daddy said, "No way! God's been too good! There's a baby named Fredricc Gerard on the way!" And here I am. I'm here to let you know that He's been too good! And I can't forget it!

I don't know what your testimony is, but you ought to just high 5 somebody and tell 'em, "He did________and I can't forget it!" Fill in the blank with YOUR testimony! "He did it and I can't forget it!"

I can't wrap this up before I tell you about Mama June. Mama June is my good friend's 90 year old grandmother. She lives in an assisted living facility because she has been diagnosed with severe dementia. A few weeks ago, I had occasion to meet Mama June, and during our hour long visit, I found myself having to remind Mama June of my name a number of times. However, something incredible happened when Mama June asked me to sing "Amazing Grace." As I began to hum and then sing the chorus, Mama June jumped in and started singing, "I once was lost but now I'm found, was blind but now I see."

You see, the grace of God had such a great impact on Mama June's life that not even the debilitating effects of dementia could make her forget it. Dear brother or sister in Christ, you've traveled the pages of these twenty sermons with us. My prayer is that somewhere along this journey, the Good Lord has spoken a word or two directly to you, from Him. Our God is big like that. He saw the readers of this book before we even thought to compile our thoughts. Thank you for taking the time. And we will leave you with this exhortation from one brother in Christ to a fellow Christ-follower: Never forget what God has done for you. Make a choice to live chosen!

Closing Prayer:

Lord, Thank You for walking with me as we journeyed from chapter to chapter. I commit my life to be a witness for You. I'll boldly tell my own story of redemption so that Heaven will be populated and hell will be devastated. All glory and honor belong to You. In Jesus' name, Amen.

About the Authors

Fredricc Gerard Brock, D.Min. (ABD) is an ordained minister and currently serves as a Chaplain, Captain in the United States Air Force Reserve. He is the co-founder, along with his beautiful wife Kan'Dace, of FGB Ministries, LLC. Through this ministry, they've traveled the country using their dynamic ministry gifts for God's glory. He is an honors graduate of Texas Southern University, with a B.S. in Health Administration, where he was also a decorated football player. He also spent time as a linebacker with the NFL's Houston Texans. He earned a Master of Divinity degree in Theology from Baylor University's George W. Truett Theological Seminary and is a candidate for the Doctor of Ministry degree at the Oblate School of Theology.

Kan'Dace Len "Lady K" Brock, LMSW is a licensed minister and currently works as a mental health counselor in San Antonio, Texas. She uses her gifts as a dynamic preacher, compassionate mental health counselor, and innovative ministry consultant to advance the Kingdom of God, for His glory. She earned her Master of Social Work degree, with a clinical concentration, from Norfolk State University and is an honors graduate of the University of Texas at Arlington, holding dual bachelor's degrees in social work and sociology. As an entrepreneur, she is also the CEO of Lilly Len's Creations and co-founder of FGB Ministries, LLC. She is currently pursuing a Master of Divinity in African American Pastoral Leadership at the Oblate School of Theology.